D0121452

THE ROYAL AND ANCIENT

HER MAJESTY QUEEN ELIZABETH II, PATRON OF THE CLUB

THE ROYAL AND ANCIENT

PAT WARD-THOMAS

Published for

THE ROYAL AND ANCIENT GOLF CLUB
OF ST ANDREWS, FIFE

by the

SCOTTISH ACADEMIC PRESS

EDINBURGH

1980

Published by
SCOTTISH ACADEMIC PRESS LTD
33 Montgomery Street
Edinburgh EH7 5JX

SBN 7073 0260 9

Printed in Great Britain by
R. & R. Clark Ltd, Edinburgh

CONTENTS

LIST OF ILLUSTRATIONS

FOREWORD

Some surprise may be expressed that the Royal and Ancient Golf Club of St Andrews should have commissioned a fresh history of the Club less than 25 years after the publication of Dr J. B. Salmond's *The Story of the R. & A.* I firmly believe, however, that these years may prove to have been among the most important in the Club's long history and that it was a wise decision that they be chronicled before memories grow dim or are extinguished. The R. & A. has been fortunate in persuading Mr Ward-Thomas to undertake this task; as a Member of the Club, he understands the unique rôle it plays in the world of golf, its long and cherished traditions and the curious, and sometimes difficult, relationship between its functions as a private Club, as the organiser of championships and as a world-wide Governing Authority; as a golf writer of distinction over many years, he is also a shrewd and knowledgable observer of the wider golfing scene.

In the context of the R. & A's history the most striking development over the past 25 years has been the astonishing growth of the Open Championship in both size and stature. While this has been fostered by a deliberate policy on the part of the Club's Championship Committee, other factors have contributed, as Mr Ward-Thomas has been quick to point out; the loyalty of such great players as Arnold Palmer and Jack Nicklaus, the impact of television and the ever-increasing popularity of the game, especially on the continent of Europe and in the Far East. Less spectacular, but no less significant, have been the growing interest in the Rules of Golf and Amateur Status, with greater emphasis on the need for continuous consultation on these matters amongst all those concerned with the administration of golf, and the new commercial pressures which have made essential a tighter control over the design of clubs and balls.

All these developments have been faithfully recorded, but Mr Ward-Thomas has not been content to give us the bare facts; in each case he has gone back to the beginning and shown us the steps by which the present position was reached. Not every development was a logical progression − accident played its part − and not every decision of the Royal and Ancient was, when viewed in hindsight, well judged. Mr

Ward-Thomas is not one of Burke's 'gentle historians' who 'dip their pens in nothing but the milk of human kindness'; on occasion he is frankly, and properly, critical of the way in which the Club has handled certain issues. Of the remoter past, however, he speaks with true affection, and the great men — members, players and professionals — live again in his pages.

There is one special reason why this history should have been written at this time. A social revolution has led to the questioning of traditional values and established authority in many areas, and golf has been no exception. It is important that the position of the R. & A. should be understood and the way in which it is adapting itself to modern conditions appreciated.

If I may end on a lighter note, not everyone is aware of these things. The Northumberland Union of Golf Clubs was consulted recently about a local rule which the Local Authority wished to introduce at one of the courses for which it was responsible. When the Union pointed out that the proposed rule contravened the Rules of Golf and that the approval of the R. & A. would therefore have to be sought, a local government official said, 'Ah! You mean the Recreation and Amenities Department.' *O sancta simplicitas*!

J. Stewart Lawson

INTRODUCTION

The origins of golf are obscure. Whether it evolved from the Roman game of paganica, kolven in Holland or other pastimes few would dispute that St. Andrews has long been the home of golf. For centuries the aged city has been renowned as a seat of learning and religion but to golfers the Royal and Ancient Club and the Old Course are the heart of its fame. No place on earth where a game is played has attracted more pilgrims and no other golf club has as many members from so many countries, nor as great an influence on the game.

The Royal and Ancient is a unique institution. It is a private members Club but has no course of its own. At the same time it is a governing body with supreme authority for the Rules of Golf, the organisation of the Open and Amateur Championships, and numerous other international affairs.

At any Autumn or Spring Meeting of the Club golfers gather from the far places of the world; the fires in the Big Room glow and the pictures of famous men look down upon the lively scene. The originals of of the portraits might be suprised to find that claret is no longer a common beverage, and meals are not banquets.

On quiet days when nothing of moment is afoot and a few members drowse in their deep chairs one might look through the tall windows and dream awhile. So peaceful is the scene, so silent the room that it is hard to believe that almost every great golfer in the game's history has stood on the tee below and looked down the long fall of fairway to the hills beyond; and that on an upper floor the processes of guidance and government are constantly under way.

The Club's stature in the game was an accident of history. Had the Old Course not existed early in the 18th century, in whatever primitive a form, the Club might never have come to life. There would have been no cause for the historic meeting on May 14, 1754 when twenty-two Noblemen and Gentlemen assembled, doubtless over a substantial repast. Admiring the game as a healthy exercise, and having the interest and prosperity of their ancient city at heart, they decided to contribute five shillings each for a Silver Club to be competed for every year. The St. Andrews Society of Golfers, subsequently the Royal and Ancient Club, was born, but the progenitors could not have imagined what would grow from the tiny seed of their inspiration.

For a hundred years and more after its foundation the Society had no particular powers. It was content to follow the original code of rules which had been devised in 1744 by the Company of Gentlemen Golfers in Leith, but when the fortunes of that Society fell into temporary decline in the 1830's there was a gradual growth of the Club's influence. Eventually, out of more than fifty countries, the United States and Mexico alone did not take their lead from the Royal and Ancient in matters of the Rules of Golf and of Amateur Status.

Of the millions who watch the Open Championship every year many are unaware that its promotion and organisation are solely the province of the Royal and Ancient. No professional golfing body is involved in any way. The Championship Committee, composed entirely of amateur golfers and assisted by a small club staff under the Secretary, bears the whole responsibility for the success or failure of an event which has become a substantial business undertaking.

The profit from the Open or other activities is devoted to the general welfare of golf and not shared among its members. For generations the Club has been a trustee for the game, its spirit and its customs. By using powers to guide rather than to dictate an effective form of democratic authority has grown. There have been no threats to the Club's stature from without, and no lasting turmoil within. It has moved peacefully into its third century, its foundations as secure as those of the grey stone Clubhouse.

CHAPTER ONE

THE COURSES

For generations golfers have journeyed from afar to visit the Royal and Ancient Clubhouse and meet the timeless challenge of the Old Course. Throughout the ages it has tested the finest golfers, all save Hogan who, alone of the great masters, never competed there. And, particularly for golfers from overseas, there is a special satisfaction in being able to say that they have been in the Club and played the course, no matter how many strokes it may have cost them. For many the experience could match a garden party at Buckingham Palace or an audience with the Pope.

The visitor will not readily forget the first impression of the place — so intimate are its policies on the very fringe of the old university city. The clubhouse, massively implanted, sombre and yet serene, is at the crest of a quadrangle, encompassing the first and last holes, flowing down to the Swilcan Burn and the long ribbon of the links beyond. On the one hand shops, houses, hotels and golf clubs form a grey terrace; on the other a vast putting green rolls towards the curve of the bay where the tide trails its silver chains. The prospect could not fail to quicken the heart of any golfer as he faces a test the like of which he will find nowhere else.

The Old Course has no parallel anywhere because its fashioning owes more to nature than to the hand of man. In the beginning there was no plan, no architect; the holes simply evolved and by some miracle have stood the test of time with little need for change except for occasional lengthening here and there to counter the power of modern equipment.

The shape of the course is much the same as it was centuries ago when the citizens of St. Andrews were granted the right to include golf among their pastimes. It runs over gently crumpled linksland out to the Eden estuary and then swings back along the 8th and 9th holes, giving it the shape of a billhook. Linksland, common to the coasts of Britain, was formed when the sea receded, leaving undulating wastes of sand.

I

These became resting places for birds whose droppings helped to fertilise seeds borne by the wind, and grasses, gorse and other vegetation grew. In time the links were an ideal breeding ground for rabbits and other animals who wore paths and burrows in the wilderness. Over the years the passage of man widened the paths and when the golfers appeared they found natural fairways, sites for greens and bunkers in profusion. At St. Andrews the space between the arable land to the south with its protective banks of whins, and the whins on the other side was so narrow, about 40 yards, that the golfers had to share the same fairways and holes going out and coming home. At first they took the left-hand route going out and returned on the other side, changing about to add variety. The left-hand route was used for the Amateur championship in 1886 and occasionally in recent years for a winter competition at a time when the Course is being rested.

The early golfers started from a tee west of the present 18th green and played to the 17th. This must have been a formidable hole. The land which now lies to the north, with its embankment and putting courses, had not then been reclaimed from the sea wherein a sliced tee shot could easily vanish. The present first green was made in 1870, some years after Tom Morris had created the 18th, the green which now bears his name.

Long ago the gorse was thinned and cut back but the Old Course, running between the Eden and the New courses, rarely measures more than 100 yards across, and its total area must be the smallest of any championship course in the world. All the while golfers cannot help but trespass on each other's fairways and indeed on the seven double greens introduced in 1832. Only the 1st, 9th, 17th and 18th have a green to themselves; the remainder are huge, rippling surfaces, some almost an acre in area. Many are on plateaus, a providential blessing, starkly exposed to the elements and fearsome places for the man whose putting touch is amiss. As Nicklaus remarked once, 'You can feel so lonely out there, missing a short putt'. Nowhere does the classic excuse for an indifferent score, that of taking three putts, sound less convincing. The golfer may find green after green, although not always his own, and leave himself putting from 30 yards and sometimes much further. Judgement of distance is of the essence in scoring well unless the player can survive a great burden on his short game. However well a man may think he knows the holes there are times when he can be far out in his reckoning. The undulating land often makes the flags look much nearer than they are.

The legend of the 'Old' as a capricious mistress, all deceitful wiles, is less true than it was before the age of watering. When the ground was baked hard and the ball running fast, short approaches needed the utmost delicacy of touch, and the little slopes and falls had to be studied and known. There was too no question of firing approaches to pitch near the flags. The course still demands unceasing vigilance and rarely does it forgive thoughtless attack, faint-heartedness or lack of perception.

The winds can be flirtatious with the movement of the tides, so much so that it is possible to play out against the breeze and face it again coming home, but it is the subtler changes of angle that can alter strategy. Within the hour, or even minutes, what was a safe line can become a dangerous one mainly because of the bunkers. They are nowhere near as plentiful as when they were holes from which sea shells were dug or places for sheep to shelter, but they are numerous enough to dictate the strategy of play on every hole, save the first and last, and to tantalise the golfer. Many are not at once visible to the striker and can be totally unexpected hazards for those ignorant of their presence. Thus contentment can swiftly turn to fury and frustration. And yet, Thomas H. Peter, in his reminiscences was moved almost a century ago to declare that 'Bunkers which gave such interest in old times now scarcely form hazards at all'. They must have been fearsome.

Any impression of innocence that the opening hole may give is swiftly dispelled by the decision as to which club is needed to carry the Swilcan Burn, revealed only by a thin dark line and further away than it looks, or whether to play short. There are no safety routes for the fearful; if the course is to be played the Burn must be crossed. The inviting expanse of green lies immediately beyond it and legion are the tales of those who have suffered sixes, sevens and worse simply because of a shallow stream some eight feet wide which becomes the more alarming the closer one is to it. Not everyone is as fortunate as the American professional who, in an Open championship, overhit his approach to the back of the green, putted down the hill into the Burn, lifted and dropped on the far side and chipped into the hole for a five.

The classic advice, echoed down the ages, to anyone in doubt as to the line from the tees is to play left rather than right, where on almost every hole the greater trouble lies, but when discretion is overdone problems arise. The next seven holes prove the point. Approaching the 2nd from the left involves carrying a deep bunker on the line to the flag with the green falling away from the shot. The only reasonable line is from the right, especially in the prevailing left-hand or contrary wind, but if the drive errs to that side bunkers and gorse await. Otherwise the sensible golfer aims for the right edge of the plateau and hopes to get down in two.

The bunkers on the right flank of the 2nd fairway and the ones similarly placed on the next three holes, as well as those on the 9th fairway, were made at the turn of the century. They are rare instances of new hazards being added to the course but they probably took the place of great banks of whins. The 4th, partly because of its length, is the toughest par on the outward journey but it was harder when one had to drive along the ridge to the left of the present fairway valley. This was an instance of how narrow the course once was, and how difficult the game must have been.

It was there at the 4th that Nicklaus came nearest to dropping a stroke in his last round in the 1978 Open. His drive finished in thick rough at the foot of the ridge. He could only play out well short of the green but pitched close and made his four. In 1930 Jones, having pulled his drive into the Cottage bunker, holed his second shot of some 160 yards. He had started 3–4–3 which was as well for S. Roper from Nottingham, proved an uncommonly resolute opponent. He played fifteen holes in four apiece. The hole is known as 'Ginger Beer' from the days when a character called 'Old Daw' used to offer refreshment there and, in summer, at the 9th. Many must have mourned his passing.

In his *Reminiscences of Golf on St. Andrews Links* James Balfour wrote that the 5th 'had been altered more than any other on the links and sadly destroyed. The tee stroke used always to be played to the right of the big bunker with the uncouth name (Hell) unless some huge driver swiped over H—— at one immortal blow'. The second was played on to the Elysian Fields and the third had to negotiate the Beardies and carry a 'wide staring bunker'. Balfour considered the 5th the finest hole on the links, possibly in the world. This is no longer true but it is fairly formidable nonetheless.

A sequence of bunkers, unseen from the tee, threaten the drive aimed at the distant flag, safety ensured, the player must decide whether he can thread the line between twin guardian bunkers and carry the hill which protects the approach to the green. The bunkers were about 420 yards from the tee in the 1933 Open when Craig Wood, with a gale behind him and the turf hard as glass, actually drove into one of them. Those who play short of the hill must remember that the next shot is a deal further than it looks.

The pin at the 6th looks temptingly close to the bank in front of the green, a clear invitation to underclub but a hidden channel intervenes.

Few low scores have been made on the Old Course without the help of the Loop and its opportunity to make six threes. It contains the only two short holes and, except for the 7th where the great Shell bunker prevents such liberties, the greens of the others have frequently been driven. In his first round in the 1921 Open Jock Hutchison holed in one at the 8th and failed by inches to do so at the 9th. The Loop can be the insurance against what is to come but it is by no means all plain sailing.

The 11th can be a fiendish short hole. According to the wind the shot may be anything between a wood and a long pitch and run. Even in calm air it is never easy with the green leaning quite steeply towards the tee, the flag behind the menacing little Strath bunker and Hill bunker on the left. If the tee shot finishes above the hole, and the green is fast with a breeze off the Eden it is alarmingly possible to putt off the green.

In 1933 Gene Sarazen was making a good defence of the Open when he pulled into Hill, from where he took three strokes to emerge, and holed out in six. Although his marker, a well-known Scottish lady player, confirmed this a steward who, apparently, could not see into the bunker from where he stood claimed that Sarazen had taken seven. Sarazen recalls the incident in his absorbing book *Thirty Years of Championship Golf.* After his second failure in the bunker he waved his club in anger. The steward, who had no right to interfere, thought it was a stroke and reported thus to the Championship Committee. Although the marker had signed his card Sarazen was summoned before the Committee, 'twelve men sitting austerely around a long table' and seemingly prepared to take the word of the steward before those of Sarazen and his marker. However Sarazen's word was accepted but he was sorely disturbed that his integrity had been doubted.

If ever a simple looking hole concealed all manner of evil it must be the 12th where the fairway is peppered with bunkers invisible from the tee. Some are only large enough for 'an angry man and his niblick', as Bernard Darwin once remarked, but one is large and deep. The tale is told of Rear Admiral C. H. G. Benson who, on leaving the tee, espied a trim feminine figure on the nearby 7th fairway. Unwisely he did not avert his gaze in time to see the bunker and suddenly vanished, keel over masthead, trolley-cart, clubs and all from sight of his companions. The Admiral, an erect, impressive figure even deep into his eighties, rarely missed a Meeting and nothing deterred him from his golf. Against advice when he was approaching ninety he insisted on playing in vicious weather and went round in 128 but the effort probably hastened his death in 1974. Some years previously the indomitable Admiral had returned a net medal score below his age. In 1958 the Admiral, H. Craufurd Benson and R. J. Craufurd Benson presented a barograph to the Club to mark 100 years of continuous membership by the family.

A safe tee shot to the 12th still leaves a teasing little stroke to a shallow oblong plateau green which in a helping wind is drivable. At a crucial stage of the Amateur championship final in 1958 Joe Carr reached the edge of the green with his tee shot and holed an enormous putt for a two. His next drive was in the Cat's Trap bunker from where he hit a seemingly impossible stroke, cutting up a four iron to the green some 150 yards away. These brutal thrusts gave him lasting command of Alan Thirlwell.

The 14th and 17th are the ultimate bastions of the course's defence against plunder. Countless golfers have left the 13th with their scores in excellent shape only to be arrested by either or both of these incomparable holes. The drive to the 14th, especially from the championship tee, makes a fearsome play on courage and technique. The paramount thought is to avoid going out of bounds over the low greystone wall which angles sharply into the line, and separates the Old from the Eden course, but only a slight pull can be trapped by the Beardies, a threatening cluster of bunkers scarcely visible from the tee. For most golfers there is no greater sense of relief on the Old Course than to see the drive finishing safely on the lovely sweep of fairway known as the Elysian Fields.

Thereafter the wind and the strength of the player dictate strategy. The long carry over Hell bunker and its attendant Kitchen may be attempted at some risk. The safe line is to the left. It then remains to negotiate the approach to a green protected by a smooth, steep bank. Few holes in golf make it as easy for the player to take six or seven without hitting a false stroke as this one does. It has humbled the finest. In 1939 Bobby Locke attempted overmuch from out of the Beardies after a great start in the first round of the Open. Fear of them the next day caused him to drive out of bounds and his two visits to the hole had cost him fifteen strokes. As mentioned elsewhere Sarazen lost the 1933 Open by being too ambitious in Hell bunker. Both these tragic lapses, and scores of others besides, emphasise a primary lesson of the Old Course. When in a bunker make certain of escape before thinking of length.

The 15th is akin to a breathing space, its problems plain to see. One is the lonely little Sutherland bunker, an infuriating place to be trapped from a solid hit. One Committee long ago decreed that it should be filled in, and this was done, but in the darkness of night it was opened again and thus it remains. Two little mounds on the fairway are known as Miss Granger's bosom and Members who are aware of the lady respectfully walk to either side.

Only the brave or unintentional shot from the 16th tee takes the line once described as 'strictly for amateurs', between the old railway fence marking out of bounds and the Principal's Nose. Once on a time when the sadly vanished railway was there it was not out of bounds and track irons were provided for purposes of extraction. Nowadays the wise drive to the left but if overdone the problem of avoiding the Wig bunker on the front corner of the green becomes all the greater. On his way to victory in the 1905 Open James Braid drove on to the railway at the 15th and took six. His drive to the 16th finished in the Principal's Nose from where, in attempting overmuch, his ball came to rest against a rail. His anxiety can be imagined as he took two shots to reach the fairway but a brave run-up shot enabled him to hole out in six. The crisis was past and he won by five strokes.

No hole on any championship course in Britain can pose the question of whether to attack or not more vividly than the Road Hole, undeniably the most famous 17th in the world. It has caused more grief and anxiety, even to the greatest golfers, than any other. Often enough the drive answers part of the question. Unless it takes a line over the corner of the hotel grounds where once black railway sheds stood the attempt to reach the green with the next shot is beset with peril. Palmer knew this well enough in 1978 when he spoiled successive good rounds by driving out of bounds. As many bemoaned the disappearance of the sheds as had opposed their construction, not for their intrinsic beauty but because they were much less alien to the scene than the new hotel. When this was being completed British Transport Hotels sought permission to call the building the Royal and Ancient. The Scottish Office did not hesitate to advise the Sovereign that this title belonged already to another organisation which would not take kindly to being confused with innkeepers, ostlers, etc. Permission therefore was refused.

The further left the drive to the 17th the tighter becomes the line to the narrow plateau of green, and if playing from the rough which can snare a pull the Scholars and Progressing bunkers enter the reckoning. The sensible approach is to aim to be on the right side of the fairway, short of the front slope of the green and to beware of the overhit shot which can finish on the road beyond. The villain of the whole piece is the infamous little Road bunker into which the shortest of approaches, even with a putter, can curl if not on the precise line. For competitions the pin is between the bunker and the road and the margin of error for the sand shot is minute. There is nothing, no little bank or fringe of grass, to stop the slightest overhit trickling on to the road.

Many memorable shots have been played from or over the Road bunker under severe pressure. One by Cyril Tolley, had Bobby Jones not been fortunate with his second shot, might have ended the 'Grand Slam' odyssey almost before it began. In 1970 Sanders played the most delicate of splash shots to the holeside in the fourth round, a stroke which should have won him the Open. Innumerable golfers have failed to escape at their first, second or even third attempt. In 1978 millions saw an impassive Nakajima play one gentle, fractionally underhit shot after another until the fourth reached the green. Thereafter caddies referred to the bunker as 'The sands of Nakajima'. The hole can be infinitely cruel and unless the making of a four be absolutely essential the vast majority of golfers will be content, even relieved, to have played it in five.

A birdie there is pure gold, if rare gold at that, and particularly if it is followed by an eagle. This was the happy fate of Graham Marsh, an admirable Australian golfer, in a professional tournament in 1973. With a strong helping wind Marsh needed only an eight iron for his second to the 17th. He holed for a three from twelve feet, and from as many yards after driving the last green. No-one present could recall anyone playing the last two holes in five strokes in a tournament. The feat launched Marsh to an easy victory the next day.

The Old Course has aroused strong emotions from dislike to enduring affection. Some golfers have lost patience with it and have not been prepared to appreciate its subtleties, the variety of its challenge, and its charm. It is a course where joy can swiftly turn to agony and despair. The reverse is also true and those who strive to understand the place usually admit that the balance is just, and that, however humble their talents may be, the golf can be infinitely rewarding.

Ownership of the Links and creation of new courses

Towards the end of the 19th century the Town Council of St. Andrews, ever anxious to preserve the citizens' rights on the links, asked the Royal and Ancient to curtail golf during the four summer months on the land between the Clubhouse and Grannie Clark's Wynd, the road crossing the first and last fairways. It was suggested by some that the course should begin on the Swilcan side of the road, and that the land towards the Clubhouse be made into a public park, with a part which could be flooded for skating.

The Club were not enamoured of these proposals and as, in any event, the Old Course was increasingly in demand they considered the making of another course for their own use, with certain privileges for non-members.

For generations the links were owned by the Cheape family of Strathtyrum but in 1890 James Cheape informed the Club that he was willing to sell. The Club naturally were pleased and made an offer of £3000 with the condition that Cheape should pay the Club £60 a year until the expiration of the then tenant's lease. Cheape declined these terms but promised that should he change his mind the Club would have first refusal.

There the matter rested for two years and then the Town Council suggested they might share ownership of a new course with the Club. At the same time they admitted that such an arrangement would mean that the course had to be public. The Club, however, were anxious to reserve a new course for their Members and offered Cheape £5000 for the property. He agreed provided, among other conditions, that he had the right, which his descendants retain, to dig for shells near the mouth of the Eden; that no buildings other than shelters for golfers be erected on the links, and that his family and guests could play on the course.

In 1893 the Club became owners of the links but the Town Council were not happy and decided to promote a Bill in Parliament to acquire them. The Club petitioned against the Bill; various adjustments were made, and in 1894 the St. Andrews Links Act was passed. The outcome was that the Burgh of St. Andrews were to hold the links as a public recreation ground and that the Club would maintain the Old Course and lay out the New. Provision was also made that the Old would always be free to the public but that it could be closed for not more than one month in a year. The New course was opened in 1895 but less than £2000 had been spent on its design and maintenance. Such was its poor condition that the Green Committee were empowered to borrow money for its improvement but such costs were rising.

Within twenty years the maintenance of both courses was more than treble the original cost. After considerable discussion a new Agreement was made with the Town Council who were well aware of the growing popularity of the game and its value to the town. They proposed to increase the facilities by developing the Jubilee course and creating another one, the Eden, designed by H. C. Colt, which was opened in 1912; and also to charge fees.

The Jubilee had been opened in 1897 on the day when Queen Victoria's Diamond Jubilee was celebrated, but it was regarded as the Ladies Course, an alternative to the gentler challenge of the Ladies Putting Green. In 1912 this course was extended from 12 to 18 holes and in 1939 Willie Auchterlonie, the Club Professional, with the aid of a few men began its reconstruction. By 1946 they had made a pleasing course on the bayside of the dunes, not over demanding but ideal for beginners and high handicap players.

If the New Course had not been the closest possible neighbour to the Old, and thereby vulnerable to comparison, it would be assured of a higher place among Scottish links than it perhaps has now. The New shares some of the Old's natural features in the quietly undulating land and appealing dune country down by the Eden. Some holes make considerable use of gorse as a hazard. Elsewhere the golf is pleasantly open but not without challenge, even though this is not as exacting of thought and control as it is across the way.

The problem of finance for the Old and New Courses persisted between the Wars. In March 1945 the Emergency Committee calculated that a minimum of £4500 would be needed and that this was beyond the Club's resources. Legally, it appeared that the 1894 Act did not compel the Club to bear the heavy costs involved in maintaining the courses to the highest pitch of condition. The Town Council were approached and took out a Provisional Order which would give them powers to contribute to the expenditure, and to charge ratepayers for their golf. Late in 1946 the Provisional Order became law. For a while thereafter Members, who were municipal voters, found themselves paying the same charges as non-members, but eventually these were waived.

For some years after the Act the Town Council contributed towards the cost of the courses. Then in 1953 the Council and the Club agreed that the most efficient and economical way of managing all four courses would be to appoint a Joint Links Committee, consisting of an equal number of Town Council and Royal and Ancient Club members.

Control of Courses

The five courses at St. Andrews are open to all golfers. No introduction is needed; anyone may play on payment of the green fee. In 1979 this was £5 a round on the Old Course, and substantially less on the New, Eden or Jubilee. Golf is free on the nine hole Balgove course which was opened in 1972 with children and beginners mostly in mind. Every year upwards of 40,000 rounds are played on the Old and almost three times as many overall on the other three.

The control of the Links as a whole, which is owned by the District Council, is vested in the St. Andrews Links Trust and the Management Committee. These bodies, on which the Royal and Ancient and the local authority are equally represented, were formed as a result of the Links Order Confirmation Act in 1974.

The Act came about as a result of the re-organisation of local government in Scotland. The Club and Town Council wisely foresaw that the links would come under the control of a more remote and widespread authority, and that this might be unsatisfactory. In May 1971 Donald Smith, Chairman of the General Committee, sent a memorandum to Sir Robert Speed, Speaker's Counsel in the House of Commons, out-lining proposals for creating a Links Trust and seeking advice as to procedure for obtaining the necessary legislation. He stressed the impor-tance of action before the Wheatley proposals for local government re-organisation were implemented.

Later that summer the General Purposes Committee of the Town Council agreed to the principle of setting up a Trust as proposed by the Royal and Ancient. Accordingly, in November 1972 the Council made application for a Provisional Order. The main purposes of the Order were to form the Links Trust and Management Committee, to protect the rights of Alexander Cheape and his successors, and to repeal the St. Andrews Links Act of 1894 and various subsequent orders.

The main responsibility of the Trust is to maintain the Links as a place of public recreation and in this light may have far reaching de-cisions to make in the near future. Facilities for golfers who are not members of one of the St. Andrews clubs are sorely needed.

The Management Committee looks after the detailed care of the courses. It can close any or part of them for rest or repair but not for longer than one month in a year. No more than two courses can be closed at the same time and the Old and New are always open during July, August and September. Traditionally the Old is left in peace on Sundays, an essential respite considering the enormous traffic it bears. For championships the courses may be closed for not more than fourteen consecutive days.

By these means the interests of the public, and visitors who play almost a third of the rounds in a year, are protected while the Royal and Ancient makes a substantial contribution to the cause. In return its

Members may play free on any course. Other privileges include the right to alternate starting times on the New except on Sundays, and preferred times on the Old in August and September, and during the weeks of the Spring and Autumn meetings. After many turns of fortune and several Acts of Parliament an equitable form of administration has evolved.

CHAPTER TWO

CAPTAINS, COMPETITIONS

Introduction

There is no more signal honour in golf than to be Captain of the Royal and Ancient. He is the living symbol of the Club's authority and guidance. There are no specific qualifications when the past Captains make their choice. The candidate may be a distinguished golfer or one of no consequence; he may be an eminent person in a field remote from golf or quite unknown to the public. As often as not he will have given notable service to the Club, and thereby the game, through work on various committees or in other respects. Whatever his stature his personal qualities are probably the paramount consideration. During his year, which can be onerous and expensive, he represents the Club and sometimes the country at home and abroad, but he has no executive duties. The number of functions he attends is partly a matter of his own conscience. That of most recent Captains is rarely satisfied with fewer than thirty or more.

The nomination of the Captain is secret until his name is announced at the Spring Meeting in May, and his succession begins on the last day of the Autumn Meeting. Early on a September morning the outgoing Captain will escort him down the steps to the first tee for the ancient ritual of driving into office. It dates from deep in the last century and is no slight ordeal for the victim. This is the one time in his life when he most dreads making a poor stroke. For many months since the former Captains elected him he has lived with the knowledge that, come the Autumn, he will have to hit one shot; there will be no second chance. Save to the golfer himself its outcome does not matter. Only his pride is at stake but pride can be a powerful factor. Custom has it that the outgoing Captain offers his successor a 'stiffener' before they leave the Clubhouse but not all have accepted, fearing perhaps that the effect might be adverse and preferring to trust to a swing that has usually served them well.

As 8 o'clock approaches a couple of hundred or so gather on the terrace before the great windows of the Clubhouse and the past Captains, usually about sixteen, assemble by the tee while Laurie Auchterlonie, Honorary Professional to the Club and son of the Open champion of 1893, asks the striker whether he would like a high, low or medium tee and adjusts it accordingly. Meanwhile the caddies, possibly a score, station themselves down the fairway. Each is hopeful of capturing the ball for the lucky one receives a gold sovereign from the new Captain. This has long been the custom and occasionally the Captain has bought the sovereign back but the value of sovereigns has soared, £38 in 1979 and most caddies of late have kept their prize. In 1951 when Francis Ouimet was Captain he gave the caddie a $10 gold coin.

The very instant after the Captain has struck his drive a cannon is fired to let everyone know that the links is closed to all but the competitors. When play has finished, and this could be the following day after a play-off for the William IV or Club Gold Medal; it is fired again and the links is a public place once more. At various times the cannon has been replaced because it was considered dangerous. The original one had been bought in 1837 from a Prussian captain for £2. In 1892 another was bought for £2 10s., prices having risen, from Sergeant Major McKee of the Royal Artillery. How long the present piece will survive is uncertain but Keith Mackenzie, the Club Secretary, who is in attendance at the moment of firing, certainly keeps a wary eye on it.

The prospect for the Captain is no easier because the long green fall to the Swilcan Burn is the widest fairway in Christendom. If he is not an expert golfer it has been known for a caddie to anticipate a mishit but such irreverence is rare nowadays. An absolute silence descends as Auchterlonie tees the ball and the watchers wait, a blend of hope and envy in their hearts. At such a moment even the most distinguished of golfers must have prayed to themselves that their swing be unhurried and that they will look at the ball. Perish the thought of the convulsive snatch and the horror of seeing it scuttering feebly away, a fate that has befallen some, not least two of the Royal Princes. By no means all the Captains have been golfers of repute but rarely in recent years has anyone failed to acquit himself with honour. Some have survived the ordeal in memorable fashion. Hogan himself could not have surpassed David Blair's superb stroke in 1978. His drive pierced the crystal morning air on the dead perfect line as if fired from a rifle. Very few, if any, doubted that it would be otherwise. Not many golfers of Blair's generation had a swing as pure and simple in outline, nor had greater confidence that it would function.

For several modern Captains the ceremony has been memorable aside from the honour itself. In 1964 Alec Hill confessed that when he descended the steps to the tee he cast away the 23rd cigarette he had smoked since the early hours, and Hill was a man of proven courage in the Second War, and a Walker Cup player in 1936. That year in the Amateur Championship at St. Andrews he played nine holes from the 7th tee in 28 strokes, a sequence probably without parallel. Cyril Tolley was the unfortunate victim. Throughout the years afterwards Hill remained an excellent golfer as he confirmed that day. After driving himself in with a solid shot far down the fairway he went round in 72 and won the William IV Gold Medal, the only Captain to do so since Captains have been elected. Among the numerous distinctions that befell Gerald Micklem during his long years of service to the game, one was unique when illness prevented him from driving in at the Autumn Meeting in 1968 he did so the following Spring. The search for a uniform ball was at its height when Sir Iain Stewart drove himself solidly into office with a 1.65 ball. Three years later Joseph C. Dey, the foremost golf administrator in the United States for thirty years and the second American Captain, had to face a vile wet morning. He also knew that his drive was to be televised throughout the United States. Although not a golfer of renown, Dey was a man of infinite composure and his swing did not fail him. No other Captain has had a gallery of millions; usually it is hundreds at most.

The story goes that one famous personage must have wished no-one was watching when he suffered the ultimate horror of missing the ball altogether but was saved by the presence of mind of Willie Auchterlonie who had teed the ball. Giving no sign that anything was amiss he remarked swiftly 'that was a very good practise swing, now just hit it.'

One of the bravest of all drives into office was that of G. W. Mackie, a fine Scottish golfer, in 1970. He was suffering from a mortal illness at the time but fortunately lived long enough to see the Walker Cup won the following summer.

The place is alive with memories for all that the scene has changed down the long years. A hotel has risen where black sheds made the drive to the 17th seem more uncompromising than it is now; a fence alone remains as a reminder of the railway from Leuchars. For over a century from 1846 it quickened the anticipation of arriving golfers like none other in the world as the links came into view. The Swilcan Burn, now severely, albeit neatly, contained was a broader natural stream flowing into the handsome curve of the bay which was much closer at hand than it is now. Modern University buildings stand where once there were meadows but the old grey houses flanking the last fairway have no relation to the twentieth century; and way to the west, beyond dark woods, quiet hills reach towards the skies and far distant mountains. There is still an inescapable sense of timelessness to the scene. In early morning or late evening when no golfers are abroad one can picture a little company, gathered south of where the clubhouse steps are now, about to begin the long narrow trail of eleven holes over rough untended land, beset on either hand with great banks of whins and bunkers. How eagerly they must have begun their contest for the Silver Club in 1754 but golf had been played on the links long before that Maytime day.

A charter, issued by the city in 1552, granted John Hamilton, the Archbishop of St. Andrews, licence to plant and nourish rabbits on the north part of the links by the Eden estuary, while reserving the rights of the people to play at golf, football, shooting and other pastimes. This was the first known reference to golf at St. Andrews although it had become quite popular in other parts of Scotland.

The game was not an exclusive pursuit. The early golfers enjoyed themselves in simple fashion on the links, unfettered by rules and organisation, and giving no thought to forming a club. Elaborate rules were framed for the Silver Club Competition. The winner was to be Captain of golf for the following year, and was to append a Silver ball to the Club. During his year of office he was charged with the settlement of any disputes and also with the care and inspection of the links. If these were encroached upon by roads or otherwise he could complain to the Provost and magistrates. Straightaway the golfers were alive to the problems of crowd control. They forbade coaches, chaises or other wheel machines, people on horseback or dogs of any kind from passing through the links. It may be presumed that Bailie William Landale, a local merchant, had no difficulty in concentrating on the task of winning the first competition. He was the first Captain of the St. Andrews Society of Golfers which became the Royal and Ancient Club when King William IV bestowed the title in 1834.

The following year Landale tied with James Leslie and Thomas Boswall and, as Captain, arranged the play-off for the next morning at 8 o'clock, perhaps hoping to steal an early march, but Boswall prevailed. For the first two years the Silver Club competition was decided by an involved system of holes won, but this was not satisfactory. In 1764 when William St. Clair mastered the 22 holes of the links in 121 strokes, it was decided that the first four holes should be converted into two. As the same fairways were used going out and coming home the course was reduced to eighteen holes. Thus the adoption of this number to make up a round of golf was accidental. Blackheath played over seven and Prestwick twelve, but eighteen became the norm. St. Clair's round, in effect 99 for 18 holes, was no mean feat for a man of 64 playing with feathery balls and unpromising implements, but he was an exceptional athlete. Sir Walter Scott wrote that he himself and other boys would crowd to see St. Clair 'perform feats of strength and skill in the old Scottish games of golf and archery'. St. Clair was one of the first great golfing figures. Not only did he win the Silver Club twice more at St. Andrews, but on four occasions was Captain of the Honourable Company of Edinburgh Golfers. In 1766 he had the rare distinction of heading the affairs of the St. Andrews golfers as well.

The ancient competition books of the Club, in which the bold, sweeping signatures of prosperous men attested to the winner's score and that the entry fees had been paid, reveal that in 1767 James Durham of Largo returned the remarkable total of 94. Fittingly, his portrait hangs in the Club for he was the first man to set a far horizon in scoring. During the remainder of the century only four other players broke 100 and his record stood for 86 years – an extraordinary feat considering the vast numbers who fail to match his score with all the advantages of modern equipment and a beautifully prepared links. Durham was also credited with referring to Edinburgh as 'Auld Reekie'. When the smoke over the city increased as the citizens prepared their supper he would say that it was time for bed, 'Yonder's Auld Reekie, I see, putting on her night-cap'.

One of the earliest instances of breaking the rules was in 1773 when a certain William Arnott, presumably after missing a short putt, pulled back his ball. Apparently he was not disqualified but the Captain and Society, showing a kindly tolerance towards one who had plainly suffered, decreed that the competition be played again. It happened during play for a Silver Cup. This was a new competition introduced when the Society decided that the one for the Silver Club should no longer be open and in future be restricted to Members of the Club or the Honourable Company.

The William IV Medal is the Club's foremost award at the Autumn Meeting and the Gold Medal purchased by the Club in 1806 is the prize for the runner-up. The competition for the Club Medal was started because the Society decided that there must be a real test to find the best players. The reason for this appears to have stemmed from doubt as to the procedure of the Silver Club competition. It was generally accepted that the winner was Captain for the following year but Doctor James Grierson in his *History of St. Andrews* claimed that the Captain was always determined in advance of the competition, and that the record therefore was false. Historians disagreed as to the validity of his contention but it may have been partly correct in that the 'elected' Captain alone was regarded as competing for the Silver Club, as he is in present times. If so his score was not fiction. The first Club Gold Medal was won by Walter Cook with a score of 100. He defended successfully the following year as in turn did William Oliphant, James Hunter and, on two occasions, Robert Pattullo. In 1834 Robert Oliphant with a 97 became the first man to break 100 in this competition.

Already the Society were concerned at the poor quality of their golfing jackets. It was agreed that there should be new ones, red with yellow buttons, and that the Committee's uniform should be a buff-coloured frock coat, half lapelled, the button white, and that a red cap be worn. This was not considered suitable and four years later the coat was changed to red with a dark blue velvet cape embroidered with a club and ball of silver, with two large buttons on the sleeves. One can imagine the consternation on a modern golfer's face if, during an Open championship, a figure clad thus appeared to give him a ruling.

During those early years some Captains probably thought that tenure of office was an honour without responsibility. In 1779 the Society decided otherwise. If the Captain did not attend all meetings throughout the year he had to pay two pints of claret as a fine for every one he missed. He was forgiven only if absent from Fife at the time. There was no dearth of reasons for consuming claret and the happy custom continued well into the next century. At the September meeting in 1825 a minute states, 'Which day the Captain imposed on himself a fine of a magnum of claret for failure in public duty, and imposed a similar fine on the old Captain present.' Some years afterwards five members were fined one bottle for 'reflecting on the Secretary and one for ordering hot water.'

The Secretary in question was Charles Grace whose father, Stuart, in 1781 had begun an extraordinary family record of service to the Club. It lasted with but slight intervals far into the twentieth century. When Charles Grace retired in 1836 the members presented him with a silver tray, kettle and stand to the value of 100 guineas, a handsome sum in those days. In 1842 his son, Stuart, took over as Honorary Secretary. On his retirement more than forty years later a minute of the Club stated that, 'without any remuneration or formal acknowledgement of his services he had spared no pains to advance the interests of the Club . . . involving a large expenditure of time and trouble with courtesy and kindness to all', but his work was far from finished.

When it was decided in 1884 that the secretary should be a paid appointment no suitable person was forthcoming and Grace continued on a part time basis. This did not work and in 1896 he again became Honorary Secretary until in 1900 Eliot Lockhart was appointed as the first full-time salaried secretary at £300 a year. By then Stuart Grace had been closely involved with the Club's progress for almost sixty years. Thereafter his son and grandson held the post of Honorary Treasurer. On the death of C. L. P. Grace the family had helped guide the affairs of the Club for the greater part of 200 years.

The Royal Patronage

In 1833 King William IV bestowed the designation 'Royal' on the Perth Golfing Society, the first club thus to be honoured. When Murray Belshes, who was soon to be Captain of the Club, learned of this he was spurred to action. In a letter to the King's private secretary, Sir Herbert Taylor, he expressed the earnest wish of the members that, as the King was Duke of St. Andrews, he would consent to be patron of the Club. At first the King declined because he had turned down other such requests, but the persuasive Belshes did not yield. He pointed out that his Club was almost a century older than the one at Perth, and that its membership included many from the Scottish gentry and nobility, and others from overseas. The King agreed in 1834 to become Patron and also that the Club thereafter be styled, 'The Royal and Ancient Golf Club of St. Andrews'. Three years later he presented the Club with a Gold Medal and Green Riband which is competed for at the Autumn Meeting and is the principal prize for all the competitions. Meanwhile in 1836 Murray Belshes, as if to give Royalty a hint, had presented the Club with 'The Silver Cross of St. Andrew', the premier award at the Spring Meeting.

The death of the King in 1838 did not deter Murray Belshes from his pursuit of Royal patronage. Queen Adelaide, the King's widow, and Duchess of St. Andrews, consented to become patron and presented the Queen Adelaide Medal, requesting that it be worn on all public occasions by the Captain to distinguish him from former Captains present. Nowadays the original medal is worn by the Captain only at the Club

dinner otherwise a miniature is worn whenever he is clad in his red coat
of office. The presentation of these medals brought the game to Royal
notice and occasional favour. During the following hundred years the
Prince of Wales (Edward VII), Prince Leopold, the Prince of Wales
(Edward VIII), the Duke of York (George VI) and the Duke of Kent all
became Captain.

Royal succession, as far as the Club was concerned, had been main-
tained. Queen Victoria was its patron and when the Prince of Wales
married Princess Alexandra the Club, aware that he had some knowledge
of the game, invited his patronage adding modestly that the Club played
over ground superior to any other in Britain. The Prince agreed, saying
that he intended to be Captain the following year. In 1863 the Club had
its first Royal Captain. It is unlikely that he took part in the Club's affairs
and John Whyte Melville acted for him. Neither, it seems, did the
Prince compete but, unlike some of his ancestors, he appreciated the
merits of the game. Little courses were laid out at Windsor, Sandring-
ham and Balmoral and the Prince gave prizes for golf at Biarritz and
Marienbad during his visits there. After his accession to the throne as
Edward VII in 1901 he granted his patronage to the Club. Inspired possibly by his brother's interest in the Club Prince Leopold let it be known
that he would like to join. He was admitted as an Honorary Member
and played himself in as Captain in September 1876. With a new play-
club given him by Tom Morris the Prince hit a respectable drive. He
attended the Club dinner, played some golf the next day, and the following year during the Autumn Meeting when he again attended the
Dinner and the Ball. Leopold had endeared himself to everyone by his
courtesy and kindness. Thereafter active Royal interest in the Club
ceased for almost half a century. In 1922 the arrival of the Prince of
Wales at St. Andrews for the September Meeting occasioned great excitement. At that time there was no more popular young man and his
enthusiasm for golf was famous. Straightaway he was made a Freeman
of the City. A manufacturer wanted to present the Prince with a dozen
balls and a silver box, but he could not see his way to accept. Perhaps
someone whispered a warning about amateur status!

The next morning 'some seven thousand people waited in the mist
and rain for the Prince to drive himself in. Andrew Kirkcaldy teed the
ball and when the Prince remarked that it was an awful job Kirkcaldy
told him to keep his eye on the ball.' In spite of the injunction the drive
was not very good, described by Bernard Darwin as a low ball slightly
to the left, but it made a happy man of Willie Petrie, one of the famous

Gourlay's clubmakers, who collected the ball and the sovereign. The Prince played a round on the New Course with Robert Boothby, his predecessor as Captain, and then competed in the Medal. He attended the Dinner and played two more rounds on the Old Course the next day. In December the Prince consented to sit for a portrait by Sir William Orpen who was prepared to accept whatever sum could be raised from the members, but he hoped it would be £1000. This was achieved and the portrait of the Prince, in a Fair Isle pullover and plus-fours, which he helped to make fashionable for golf, hangs on the north wall of the Big Room in the Club.

The Prince was in Canada at the time of the Autumn meeting the following year, and regretted his inability to hand over to his successor. Sir Ralph Anstruther had been appointed deputy during his year of office. The Prince presented the Club with a replica of the original Silver Club and his ball was the first to be attached to it. No more balls were added to the first two clubs.

That same year the Duke of York was invited to become an Honorary Member and in 1930 was elected Captain. The Duke, probably more naturally gifted for games than his elder brother, was a considerable lawn tennis player and had competed at Wimbledon. When the moment came to drive himself in on a fine sunny morning before a crowd of some 2000 his rhythmic swing delivered the ball 200 yards down the middle. The Duke presented a Silver Cup which, together with Henry Bethune's Victory Cup, were given by the Club to the Town Council as prizes for the Eden tournament. After playing in the Medal the Duke had an afternoon round when he was partnered by A. D. Cave, Captain in 1971 who has a special place in the Club's chronicles. In 1927 Cave had won the William IV Gold Medal; forty-one years later, when well into his sixties, he won the Club Gold Medal with a score of 71, remarkable proof of enduring skill. No Member, not even the legendary Balfour-Melville, had won two of the Club's most important Medals over such a long span.

The Duke of Kent, who was Earl of St. Andrews, followed his brothers as Captain in 1937. He lost no time in practising under the expert guidance of Archie Compston, one of the leading professionals of the day, and played a round on the New Course. Again a large crowd was in attendance as Willie Auchterlonie teed his ball the following morning, but sadly, the Duke hit the ground behind it and the drive was but modest. During the next forty years there was no other Royal Captain and at this time of writing there is no immediate prospect of one, but Her Majesty Queen Elizabeth II is Patron and in 1974 her portrait was painted for the Club by Leonard Boden.

Great Victorians and their successors

From the beginning the Members of the Club mostly were men of substance and rank, the squirearchy of the time, accustomed to authority. Several were to have an enduring place in the Club's history. Foremost among them was John Whyte Melville, the only man who was twice accepted as Captain. Sixty years after first holding office in 1823 he again accepted the nomination but died before he could take over. Furthermore he acted as deputy for the Prince of Wales when he was Captain in 1863, and twice was host to Prince Leopold during his Captaincy.

Whyte Melville was a member for 67 years and inevitably became known as Father of the Club. It is unlikely that anyone was held in as high regard, not least for his remarkable enthusiasm. It was his habit to play two rounds a day three times a week. Even when he was 83 a December gale did not deter him from his 36 holes. He was a famous 'waggler' of the club and it is possible that Herd, his caddie, may have passed the habit to his grandson, Sandy Herd, Open champion in 1902 and the most famous of 'wagglers'. The driving putter was a club often used in those days for hitting the ball low under the wind. Whyte Melville is seen to be holding one in the splendid picture which hangs in the Big Room of the Clubhouse. As long ago as 1878 it was insured against fire for £500. It also inspired these lines:

> There to the left I see Mount Melville stand
> Erect, his driving putter in his hand
> It is a club he cannot leave behind
> It worked the ball so well in the wind.

A lasting tribute to his memory is the Silver Putter to which are attached the Club's Gold Medals when they become filled with the names of the winners. It was the outcome of a wager in 1820 between Whyte Melville and Sir David Moncrieffe on the length of their lives. They agreed that the survivor would present such a putter with the arms of the two men engraved upon it. Whyte Melville outlived his friend by fifty years. The Club saw no objection to the gesture being revived in 1974 when Sir Iain Moncrieffe backed his life against that of H. H. Sykes, a descendant of Whyte Melville. The survivor was to present a pewter tankard to the Club, to be known as the Captain's Tankard.

OLD TOM MORRIS

YOUNG TOM MORRIS

Among Whyte Melville's many activities on the Club's behalf was to serve on a small committee appointed by the Prestwick Club to organise a match in 1857 between eight of the leading clubs. It was played at St. Andrews and won by Royal Blackheath, who were represented by George Glennie and J. C. Stewart, both members of the Royal and Ancient whose team they defeated in the final. In effect the contest was the birth of championship golf, as opposed to private matches which had been the invariable custom thereto. Incidentally, no provision was made in that first tournament for the settling of halved matches. In this event both teams passed into the next round, a custom preserved in the Club's competitions for the Jubilee Vase and Calcutta Cup.

In 1853 Stewart won the William IV Medal with a 90, the first man to beat James Durham's record of 94 in 1767. Stewart appears to have been a gifted, natural golfer who did not trouble to tee his ball but simply threw it down and played from wherever it landed. Two years later Glennie was victorious with an 88, a score that was to remain unbeaten until Horace Hutchinson did so in 1884. Glennie also seems to have been uncommonly talented from youth. It was said that in his student days at St. Andrews he was so much better than anyone else that his friends allowed him to use only one club. Even with a battered old mid-spoon, the equivalent of a longish iron, he still prevailed. Such was Glennie's fame and the esteem in which he was held that in 1880 the Captain of Royal Blackheath offered a Gold Medal to the Royal and Ancient. After some discussion as to its best use it was decided in 1882 that it should be awarded to the player with the lowest Medal aggregate at the Spring and Autumn meetings, and this has continued ever since. It was written of Glennie that 'none was ever imbued with a more whole-hearted devotion to the game; none ever more earnestly, if unobtrusively, upheld the integrity of its interests and traditions'.

One of the most prominent figures in the life of St. Andrews and the Club in the first half of the 19th century was Sir Hugh Lyon Playfair, a Provost of the city whose picture looks sternly down on the scene in the Big Room. His father, James Playfair, had become a Member in 1801 and was Chaplain to the Society. Its spiritual welfare was considered to be important and the appointment has continued to the present time. After a career as a soldier in India he settled to a life of social reform in St. Andrews where he had a major influence in the founding and running of the Union Club which preceded the present clubhouse as a gathering place. In 1845 Playfair presented a silver medal on behalf of the Bombay Golfing Society. This is the second prize in the Silver Cross competition. During discussions concerning the Medal someone, who must have suffered some trickery on the course, proposed that there be a three stroke penalty for 'foul' strokes. Wiser counsels prevailed. Sir Hugh was responsible for the motion in 1832 which gave a year's relief to opponents of the stymie. He must have been a considerable golfer having won the William IV and the Club Gold Medals. When he died in 1861, five years after he was Captain, the Clubhouse had been built and it was written that 'traces of the wise head and cunning hand of the Provost were to be found on the links and in the Clubhouse, as well as in every part of the ancient city'.

Medal days were momentous occasions. J. B. Salmond's researches for his *Story of the Royal and Ancient* uncovered a volume by Thomas Frognall Dibdin which gives a detailed account of the Dinner and the Ball during the Autumn Meeting in 1836. These were arranged by a Mrs Adamson of the Cross Keys where the Members had their meetings on the mornings of the Medal. Afterwards they marched to the links preceded by men carrying the Silver Club and Balls. Their arrival was announced by the firing of a cannon and play began at 11.00.

A compelling figure in the mid-nineteenth century was Samuel Messieux, a Swiss who taught French at the Madras College and achieved considerable fame as a long hitter. It was claimed that he once drove a feathery ball some 360 yards from the Hole O Cross green (13th) into Hell Bunker. The wind must have been a tempest, the ground frozen. Whether this story be true or not Messieux won the Club Gold Medal and the Silver Cross but, like many another powerful player he was 'something nervous, that's a bad affair, it sadly spoils his putting.' Nerves can have played little part in the philosophy of Captain (later Admiral) Maitland Dougall. On the day of the Autumn Medal in 1860 a tremendous gale was blowing and a ship was in distress in the bay. The lifeboat, then housed where Rusacks Hotel stands, was launched at the mouth of the Swilcan but was short of crew so Maitland Dougall, who was due to play in the Medal, took the stroke oar and spent five hours at sea. James Gourley, the famous ball-maker, who was there remarked that he would not have gone out in the boat for a thousand pounds. The men from the ship were rescued and Maitland Dougall, seemingly none the worse for the ordeal, was not to be denied his golf. He went forth into the gale and won the Club Gold Medal. The force of the wind can be gauged from the fact that his score of 112 equals the highest ever returned in either Gold Medal competition. And this in spite of having bored a hole in his ball, a gutty, and inserted buckshot so that it would fly low. He was no mean golfer for those days, having won both Medals three times, but his name lives on for a remarkable feat of endurance.

Gales have afflicted countless Medals over the centuries. One golfer, O'Brian Peter, used his driving putter for every shot in 1851 and won the William IV Medal with 105. It would be fascinating to see how a modern expert would fare in a violent wind were he restricted to one club and a gutty. Although this type of ball survived for another generation, clubs were improving, membership and competition increasing, and, as a result, scoring steadily improved. In 1869 Thomas Hodge won the William IV Medal with 89, only the second score under 90, and this heralded an age of highly accomplished players.

No name appeared more frequently in the winner's lists than that of Leslie Balfour-Melville. He won the first of his numerous Medals in 1874, and in 1895 beat the great John Ball in the final of the Amateur championship. He was a member of the first 'Rules of Golf Committee' and played in the first of all international matches in 1902 when England met Scotland at Hoylake. Bernard Darwin wrote that Balfour-Melville was an exceptional games player with a fine, orthodox swing which looked likely to last him for ever, and did endure for a very long while. His last Medal victory was not until 1908, in the Club Gold Medal and this helped him to win the Glennie Medal that year.

Among mighty golfers of the time were Horace Hutchinson, in 1908 the first English Captain of the Club, and S. Mure Fergusson who in 1893, was the first man to break the 80 barrier in a Club competition. John Laidlay and Hutchinson each won the Amateur championship twice, and Hutchinson, the author of numerous books became the most prolific of all golf writers before Darwin. These men, together with Ball, Harold Hilton and John Graham, the pride of Hoylake, Freddie Tait and Robert Maxwell, were a formidable company. No-one ever won an Amateur championship more impressively than Tait at Sandwich in 1896. In successive rounds he defeated five of his greatest contemporaries, Charles Hutchings, Laidlay, Ball, Hutchinson, and Hilton in the final by 8 and 7. Three years later he lost one of the most remarkable finals to Ball at Prestwick, a match that Darwin recalled as the most stirring he had seen. In the last autumn of the old century Tait beat John Ball over 36 holes at Lytham. This is the final entry in his golfing diary. The following year Tait was killed in the Boer War while serving with the Black Watch and this was a grievous loss to golf and to the Club. He was a hero to the Scottish crowds and indeed there was an heroic cast about him which his portrait in the Clubhouse clearly conveys.

For thirty years, until the First World War brought a long golden afternoon to an end, the foremost amateur golfers held sway as they never would in the generations that followed. Only a small company of professionals were their equal or superior as players; the age of money tournaments, apart from the Open Championship, had scarcely dawned.

Towards the end of the century the Club acquired two more trophies. Members of the Calcutta Club, founded in 1829 and the oldest in the world outside Britain, had received hospitality from the Royal and Ancient on a visit to St. Andrews. In appreciation of this they presented, in 1882, a Silver Cashmere Cup made of the silver rupees which had been subscribed for it to the tune of sixty guineas. Rather than use it as a second prize for one of the competitions the Club decided that it should be the reward for the winner of a singles handicap event, and from 1921 a foursomes event the first in the Club's history. Until 1920 the handicaps were given as holes received or owed; thereafter the usual form of stroke allowance was used.

The Calcutta Cup was followed in 1887 by a Vase to commemorate Queen Victoria's Jubilee. This is played for by singles match play under stroke handicap. Both events form the prelude to the principal competitions at the Autumn Meeting and, as in the first Amateur Championship, if a match is halved both sides pass into the next round. Occasionally this involves curiously odd numbers and byes in the later stages. In 1927 Cyril Tolley won the Jubilee Vase, having conceded over 60 strokes to his various opponents including 19 to a professor who had two of them on the 8th, the shortest hole on the Old Course. By then Tolley, together with Roger Wethered had become one of the most commanding figures in the game.

After serving in the First World War, Tolley went up to Oxford where in 1920 Wethered, four years his junior, was Captain of the University golf. He invited Tolley to play against Cambridge. He did so and Tolley was concentrating afterwards on cricket when Wethered persuaded him to go to Muirfield for the Amateur championship. Tolley had no lively expectations but his great natural power and an enchanted putter took him to the final where he beat Robert Gardner, one of the finest American golfers of the day, at the 37th hole. Wethered's turn for prominence came the following year at St. Andrews in the Open, and again in 1923 when he won the Amateur Championship at Deal, having survived a great match with Ouimet in the semi-final. He was the Captain elect in 1939 but the September meeting was cancelled and

Henry Sutherland, the retiring captain, was asked to continue until Wethered could play himself into office. Seven years later he did so, and soon afterwards played thirteen holes with General Eisenhower, one of an eminent company of soldiers, sailors and airmen who had accepted Honorary Life Memberships in recognition of their services during the war.

For a while the Captaincy alternated between men of rank and distinction in fields other than golf, and golfers of the stature of Cyril Tolley, Francis Ouimet, John Beck and William Tweddell. When Ouimet ceased to be a playing member of American Walker Cup teams he became the non-playing captain and before the match at St. Andrews in 1947 when the United States regained the trophy by 8–4 he was made an Honorary Member. No golfer was held in warmer regard than Ouimet, and his election as Captain in 1951 was a fitting tribute to his personal qualities, and also to the excellent relations with the United States Golf Association. Ouimet was the first overseas player thus to be honoured. His portrait in the Committee Room was copied by President Eisenhower from the original by Thomas E. Stephens, and presented to the Club by Bobby Jones. The portrait of Jones himself was painted for the Club from photographs by Arthur G. Mills in 1966.

Year by year entries for the competitions increased until by the late seventies some 400 were competing for the Medals with widely differing degrees of skill and enthusiasm. Even the death of a partner was no great deterrent to some. In 1948 J. F. Gilliat collapsed and died on the first fairway. His companions reluctantly continued their round after M. Crawley-Boevey had enjoined W. C. Macdonald to hurry or they would be caught for slow play.

Even in the chronicle of an ancient game two hundred years is a long time. That a Club should enjoy a growing, prosperous and unbroken existence for two centuries was a distinction that demanded unusual celebration. The birthday, May 14, fell during the Spring Meeting in 1954. One hundred and seventy-four Members attended the Dinner which was held in the Town Hall as a gesture to the past as in early years the Club had dined in the Market Street Tolbooth. John Inglis, Captain of the Club, was in the chair and among the guests was the Earl of Elgin, one of whose ancestors headed the list of the twenty-two original Members. Earlier that day James C. Wilson made his contribution to the historic occasion by winning the Silver Cross with a round of 68. Twenty-five years later his score stood alone as the lowest ever returned in a Club Medal. In the evening it was learned that

Viscount Bruce of Melbourne had been nominated as the next Captain. This was a timely choice as the most significant part of the celebration was the first Commonwealth tournament, to be held on the Old Course in June. The tournament was suggested by Gerald Micklem who proposed that instead of various Commonwealth countries, which then included South Africa, making separate tours of Britain they should combine in one event.

Most of the visiting golfers had experienced nothing like the Old Course before, but fortunately it was in sympathetic mood. The fairways were splendid, the greens easy and consistent in pace throughout and the wind, never strong, hardly varied in direction. These conditions gave the British no particular advantage but although the tournament was not a desperately earnest affair the team might have fared rather better than it did. The matches with Australia, who won their other three, and with South Africa were halved; New Zealand were narrowly beaten and on the final day the British lost to Canada. This was a little surprising from golfers as accomplished as Micklem the captain, David Blair, James Wilson, together with the powerful, handsome striking of Ian Caldwell, Frank Deighton and Alan Thirlwell.

The Australians well deserved their victory and the primary purpose of the tournament, the gathering of golfers from distant lands, was admirably achieved. When the play was done the teams and their managers were guests of the Club at another dinner in the Town Hall and silver ashtrays were presented to the members of the five teams. As a prelude the Members of the Club had the rare experience of seeing ladies drinking champagne in the Clubhouse. A strictly masculine bastion had been breached for the first time in many a long year, but by no means the last as enlightenment dawned. Afterwards a contemporary correspondent was moved to write, 'It has been a happy week and one will treasure the memory of walking out each morning in the still promise of early summer, with the clean bite of the breeze from the sea, the lovely green turf and, at the day's end, the sunset shining on the golden bay, but most of all of the atmosphere of good fellowship, friendly rivalry and humour. The Royal and Ancient can be proud of its celebration.'

Aside from the triumph at St. Andrews the Bi-Centenary year was remarkable for the success of Australian golfers in numerous other events. Douglas Bachli became the first Australian to win the Amateur championship, with an unexpected and brave victory at Muirfield over William Campbell, one of the foremost American amateurs of the generation. A month later Peter Thomson brought further glory to his country by winning the Open at Birkdale, the first of his five victories, and Peter Toogood was the leading amateur. The triumphs of Bachli and Thomson meant that the Victoria Club in Melbourne, of which both were members, enjoyed a rare distinction among overseas clubs. Only East Lake in Atlanta, where Jones was a member has housed both trophies in the same year. As if this were not sufficient unto the day for Australia, Thomson won the professional match play championship on the Old Course in the autumn; and later he and Kel Nagle won the World (then Canada) Cup for their country. It was an historic year for Australia, as well as for the Royal and Ancient.

Many fine golfers had their moments in Club affairs hereabouts. Gerald Micklem won the William IV Medal and the Silver Cross twice, and the Club Gold Medal three times. After a 70 in the Silver Cross at the Spring Meeting in 1955 David Blair became the first player to break 70 in the William IV Medal. These rounds gained him the George Glennie Medal with a total of 139 which has not been equalled. Among other distinguished names on the Medal rolls were those of Reid Jack, John Blackwell, Charles Lawrie and William Dickson Smith, who shared fifth place in the 1957 Open at St. Andrews, but Frank Deighton surpassed them all as a winner of Club competitions. Between 1953 and 1979 he won no fewer than twenty of the scratch prizes. This tally, exceeded only by Leslie Balfour-Melville, included the George Glennie Medal seven times. Although Deighton, one of the finest strikers of the period in British amateur golf, won the Scottish championship twice he did not fully justify an exceptional talent in international events. At the same time very few Members in the history of the Club approached his mastery of the Old Course.

Meanwhile further trophies had come the Club's way. The Kangaroo's Paw was presented by the Australian Golf Union as an award for the lowest net score in the Spring Medal. Previously the Royal Queensland Club had given the Silver Boomerang which performed the same service for the Autumn Medal. The Club has enjoyed a close affinity with Pine Valley in the United States and in 1966 that Club presented the Pine Valley Plate. This rewards the golfer over 55 who returns the lowest net score in the Autumn Medal. The Canadian Silver Beaver is for the net equivalent of the George Glennie Medal. It was presented by Royal and Ancient Members in Canada to mark the Canadian Centenary in 1966. In the early seventies The New Zealand Golf Association presented the Manaia Trophy for the runner-up in the Jubilee Vase and the

Australian members of the Club commemorated the Bi-Centenary of Captain Cook's discovery of their country with a Silver Trophy. In 1979 the United States Seniors Association presented the Ellis Knowles Trophy.

CHAPTER THREE

THE OPEN

On a grey evening at Carnoustie in 1953 Ben Hogan, having won the Masters and U.S. Open that year, reached an incomparable peak of achievement with victory in the Open championship. His prize was £500, a sum that would have seemed untold gold to Willie Auchterlonie who, as champion sixty years earlier, had received £30 for his triumph, but a trivial amount to Severiano Ballesteros who won £15,000 in 1979. Even allowing for inflation which had reduced the purchasing power of the pound fivefold, the difference was enormous. It is the more remarkable in that the total prize money in 1979 was over £150,000, sixty times greater than it was in Hogan's year. Three factors were primarily responsible: the increasing involvement of television throughout the golfing world, the resurrection of American interest in the Open, inspired by Arnold Palmer in the early sixties and sustained notably by Jack Nicklaus, and the good husbandry of the Royal and Ancient. The Club gradually appreciated the commercial potential of the championship and were determined that its stature should have no peer. They succeeded beyond all imagining.

In the beginning the Royal and Ancient had no part in the Open which was inspired by the Prestwick Club. In May 1860 J. O. Fairlie, a distinguished golfer who a few years later won the St. Andrews, Prestwick and North Berwick medals in the same summer, proposed that a subscription be opened to provide a medal for a professional competition. This met with no great enthusiasm from other clubs and Prestwick alone bore the responsibility for the championship. A Challenge Belt of red morocco leather was bought instead of a medal and on October 17, 1860 eight professionals played three rounds over the twelve hole links. Willie Park of Musselburgh won, beating Tom Morris by two strokes, but he was not strictly an Open champion. The event was confined to professionals. The following year Fairlie proposed that gentlemen players from St. Andrews, the Honourable Company of Edinburgh Golfers, North Berwick, Prestwick, Blackheath, Carnoustie,

Perth and Leven be allowed to compete. On the eve of the second championship it was decided that on all future occasions, unless otherwise resolved, it should be open to the world. Thus, subject to handicap qualifications for amateurs, it has remained.

One condition of the Open was that if any golfer won thrice in succession he should hold the Belt for evermore. When Young Tom Morris took possession in 1870 the rules of the championship had to be revised. After a year of reflection the Royal and Ancient received a letter from Prestwick as to the desirability of reviving the Champion Belt competition. The Green Committee were empowered to contact other clubs with a view to their joining the project. Eventually in October 1872 arrangements were complete for the Open to be played alternatively at Prestwick, Musselburgh and St. Andrews, and no less than £10 was contributed. The Clubs provided a Silver Cup, which became and is still the permanent trophy, and a gold medal for the winner. The Cup has since been duplicated, the original remaining at St. Andrews. The Open rotated between the three Clubs until 1894 when, for the first time it was played in England at Royal St. George's, Sandwich.

In 1876 the Club's organisation of the Open was desperately amiss. The Committee did not reserve times for the competitors who had to play on a course crowded with visitors, but that was not all. Approaching the 17th on the Old course David Strath learned that he needed two fives to beat Bob Martin and win. Apparently, so it was claimed by Martin's supporters, Strath had played his third before the players ahead had cleared the green, and that his ball was stopped from going on the Road. He got his five but took six at the last and tied with Martin whose friends then entered their protest. Nothing in the Rules covered such a happening which simply was a rub of the green, or at worst a breach of etiquette. Obviously no penalty was involved but the Committee met and after what must have been a dither of uncertainty ordered the tie to be played off on the Monday 'under protest'. Strath rightly took the view that the protest should be settled first otherwise, if the decision went against him, there was no point in playing. He did not appear and Martin walked the course for the Open and the £10 prize. Strath was not disqualified and received the second prize of £5. Happily, the Committee never again appeared so pathetically indecisive.

In 1892 the Open was extended to 72 holes and the following year the prize money was increased to £100, with £30 and the gold medal to the winner. According to contemporary comment this was deemed adequate reward. In 1896 Vardon was said to have received purses,

watches and a host of other substantial souvenirs which, 'coming on top
of the £30 he won at Muirfield, ought to make him into quite a rich
man. In this matter of money-making the present-day professional is far
ahead of his predecessors.' A few years earlier the professional received,
along with the bay leaves and the glory, only £10 or £12. A century
later the man in 25th place won 100 times more. J. H. Taylor was
champion in 1894 and the age of the 'Great Triumvirate' was born.
In a span of 21 years until the First World War, Vardon with six victories, Braid and Taylor with five apiece, dominated professional golf.
No-one gave much heed to the game's coming of age in the United
States until in 1913 Frances Ouimet achieved the seemingly impossible
by defeating Vardon and Ray in a play-off for the United States Open.
The American challenge for world supremacy was born. The Open
Championship forever more would cease to be a domestic event and
the Royal and Ancient would find it essential to form a Championship
Committee.

The first post-war Open at St. Andrews in 1921 brought victory to
Jock Hutchison after a play-off with Roger Wethered. Hutchison was a
native of the city but in common with hundreds of other Scottish golfers
had sought his fortune in the rich pastures of the United States and had
become an American citizen. He was fortunate that Wethered, after a
fine drive to the 18th in the last round pitched short and took five. This
allowed Hutchison to tie with a four and the next day he won with
plenty to spare. Justice probably was served because Wethered, anxious
to play cricket in the south after the Open, asked that he might have an
early starting time on the last day instead of the late one the draw had
given him. Mistakenly, the Committee agreed to a request which, as
Bernard Darwin observed, might not have been granted to a professional. Thus Wethered was able to get his blow in first which could
have been a distinct advantage for he set Hutchison a severe target. No
British amateur since has come anywhere near as close to victory.
Wethered, who was Captain of the Club in 1946, was, together with
Cyril Tolley, Captain two years later, one of the foremost amateurs of
the generation. He was Amateur champion at Deal in 1923 a year that
his sister, the greatest of all British women golfers, won one of her
numerous English championships.

While Wethered and Hutchison were trying their conclusions two
American golfers, who were to command the next decade, were passing
from the scene without distinction. On the second day Bobby Jones,
already at 19 a golfer of priceless gifts, so lost patience with himself and

the Old Course that he picked up his ball on the 11th hole, an action he
was to regret more than any other in his golfing career. Little did he
realise on that sad day that St. Andrews was to become a cherished part
of his life. Meanwhile Walter Hagen, the most vivid personality in golf
between the wars, finished a moderate sixth but he was champion the
following year. By 1930 he and Jones had won the Open seven times
between them.

Throughout the twenties the prize money remained below £500
with the champion receiving no more than £100. In 1922 it was £75
and Hagen, a man of impulsive generosity, who believed that money
was for spending and not counting, gave it all to his caddie. If the prizes
were small it was mainly because watching in those days was free.
Doubtless the Championship Committee rested easy on the belief that
victory was sufficient reward in itself, and so in the minds of men like
Hagen, Sarazen, Cotton and others it was. All made rich capital from
their victories. The Open then was regarded as having the greatest
prestige of any championship in the world, a prestige which many
believed it had regained by the seventies.

Gate money had first been charged in 1926 but in 1931 when the
Championship Committee proposed to charge at St. Andrews they were
thinking not of financial gain but of crowd control. They informed the
Town Council that they would hold an Open on the Old Course provided there were admission charges. Some months later the Committee
learned that the Council were promoting a Provisional Order, essential
because the links was on common land. This would give the Council
greater powers, including the right to charge gate money, and to close
the links during championships. The Committee were concerned that
some proposals in the Order might affect the rights of Club Members
and sought counsel's advice. Lord Cooper K.C. suggested that an Extraordinary General Meeting be called before further action was taken. The
delay proved welcome because before the meeting correspondence had
passed between the two sides who came to an amicable agreement. In
June 1932 the St. Andrews Links Order Confirmation Act was passed.
Gate money could be charged and the links closed for not more than
fourteen consecutive days or 25 days altogether in any one year.

All then was clear for the 1933 Open on the Old Course which was
won by Densmore Shute after a tie with Craig Wood. Sarazen, the
defending champion finished a stroke behind them after taking eight at
the Long Hole In, in the last round when he attempted an overly
ambitious recovery from Hell bunker. This ended a ten year sequence of

American victories. Cotton was approaching his magnificent best which reached its peak in 1937, but save this year when the whole United States Ryder Cup team competed, American interest in the Open had declined.

When the Open returned to St. Andrews in 1946 Sam Snead won but did not defend and rarely played in the championship again. There had been an interval of seven years since Richard Burton's towering pitch to Tom Morris's green had closed the door on his pursuers. This was the sixth successive British victory and after Cotton had his majestic hour at Muirfield in 1948 the Open gradually became the province of golfers from overseas, only one of whom was an American, and that was Hogan. His appearance was a unique pilgrimage, as most people imagined it would be, but it left an indelible impression. Television of golf was still some while distant, spectator facilities were minimal and there was no great arena for him to approach but the last long fairway was lined deep as thousands acclaimed the greatest golfer they had ever seen. The sight of the grey, slight figure bowing impassively, almost humbly it seemed, on the last green was unforgettable. There had been no suspense, Hogan had long since dismissed any challenge, no sudden turns of fortune simply an inexorable progress to victory. He never again competed in the Open; he had made his masterful gesture to posterity, a gesture that no-one yet has matched. Thereafter the Open pursued a quiet course while Locke and Thomson won seven times between them in nine years. Thomson almost took a five year lease on the trophy. After three successive victories he was second to Locke at St. Andrews in 1957 and won again in 1958. It was no fault of his, nor of Locke's, that the championship was losing something of its stature as a great occasion and some of its dramatic appeal. The competition simply was not strong enough.

The Royal and Ancient, who were not commercial sponsors, had no means of enticing the leading Americans to compete but were endeavouring to improve the championship wherever possible within their limited means. These could not include the provision of stands and when the matter was raised in 1958 the Committee said they could be erected provided they were the responsibility of the local club. Spectator facilities as they became known years later, were pretty basic in all respects. In 1957 N. C. Selway and his Championship Committee decided that the order of play for the final day would be pre-determined by the scores after 36 holes so that the highest were out first and the leaders last. After watching American tournaments Selway had been impressed by a method which greatly diminished the possibility of some players having an unfair advantage in changing weather conditions. Also it wellnigh guaranteed a true climax whereas there had been occasions as in 1956 when the champion had been almost determined while many others were still on the course. This was a decided boon for the spectators and revealed a consideration for them not always apparent previously. Naturally the decision was welcomed by television.

Television coverage of golf then was in its infancy and the B.B.C. were not greatly sympathetic to the idea. The planning and expense involved were far greater than for other major games which took place within a confined area. Neither at that time did the leading golfers have the appeal that would attract mass audiences. In fact the B.B.C. probably felt that they were doing golf a favour. It was agreed that in 1958 they should pay not more than £450 for one and a half hours coverage on each of the last two days, a trivial sum in the light of what was to come.

Oddly enough in 1957 television was involved in an incident without parallel in the Open. After Locke, who could win with a five on the last hole, had pitched his second to within two feet he marked his ball, moving the marker to one side so as not to interfere with the line of Crampton, who was playing with him. When Locke's turn came to putt he failed to replace the ball on its original spot and holed out. His aberration was not noticed by either Crampton or any of the watching officials, but attention was drawn to it a few days later by people who had seen it on the television film. Locke could have been disqualified but Selway and his Committee rightly decided to take no action. After seeing the film Locke was horrified when he realised that his mistake conceivably could cost him the championship and wrote to the Royal and Ancient for a decision. He was re-assured by a letter from Selway pointing out that in exceptional circumstances the Committee has the power to waive disqualifications (Rule 36 (5)). Selway ended his remarks by writing 'The Committee considers that when a competitor has three for the Open championship from two feet and then commits a technical error which brings him no possible advantage, exceptional circumstances then exist and the decision should be given, accordingly, in equity and the spirit of the game.' What an unholy clamour there would have been had the Committee decided otherwise.

The incident was the first of what might be termed trial by television. At Troon in 1973 Tony Jacklin was an unfortunate victim when he adopted the wrong dropping procedure. His action was observed on television by a Committee member and he was penalised two strokes.

By a harsh irony his mistake was prompted by a desire, as he thought, not to take an undue advantage.

When Gary Player began his remarkable span of victories in major championships no-one suspected that a golden era for the Open was just beyond the horizon. The days at Muirfield in 1959 passed peacefully enough; not a single American finished in the first twenty but Reid Jack, a most gifted Scottish amateur, shared fifth place only four strokes behind Player. No British amateur since has approached such eminence. Meanwhile in the United States formidable forces were gathering in the shape of two men who were to transform the face of the Open beyond all dreaming in the years that followed.

Not since the coming of Hogan had the appearance of a golfer in Britain quickened expectation to the extent that Palmer's did in 1960. When he arrived at St. Andrews he had already won the Masters and United States Open that summer and straightaway responded to the challenge and appeal of the Old Course. As swiftly British watchers responded to the strength and attack of his golf, and the magnetism of his personality which was to captivate the whole golfing world. The gate receipts were almost double those for 1959 and a profit of £6600 was made. Although a gallant Kel Nagle denied him victory the spell of Palmer had begun to work. When he won the next year at Birkdale the resurrection of the championship was under way but Palmer was almost frustrated. On the third day when the final 36 holes were due to be played the course was so wet that, after little more than an hour, play had to be abandoned. Tom Harvey, the Chairman, and his Committee were anxious men as they came to a decision which might have had drastic consequences. They decided that if two rounds could not be completed the following day, a Saturday, the Open would be declared void. Sunday then was considered inviolate and to hold the championship over until the Monday would cause vast inconvenience for numerous people. Palmer was not amused but did not express his dislike of the decision in public. I recall him saying that he would wait for days because he had come to win the Open. Mercifully the rains relented and win it he did. Would he have come again the following year had there been no further play? Much may have rested on the whim of the weather that Saturday at Birkdale.

The most powerful American entry since 1937 accompanied Palmer, the Pied Piper, to Troon the following year and were scattered like chaff on the wind. Such was his mastery of fast, bouncing conditions that only Nagle was within remote sight of him. His total of 276 was an Open record, matched by Tom Weiskopf eleven years later on the same course but unbeaten until Watson and Nicklaus wrought their magic at Turnberry in 1977. The final hour of Palmer's year became a salutary lesson for the Championship Committee. The control of a crowd, whose excitement over Palmer developed into an ugly stampede, proved to be quite inadequate. There was no repetition thereafter.

Although Palmer then was supreme and subject to fanatical hero-worship the foundations of his throne were beginning to tremble. That summer Nicklaus had beaten him in a play-off for the United States Open. At Troon Nicklaus finished 29 strokes behind Arnold, who scarcely spared him a backward glance, but destiny was scheming far ahead. In the next seventeen successive Opens, Nicklaus was thrice champion, second seven times and only once outside the first six.

Throughout all these years Nicklaus was always the man to beat, the standard bearer of greatness. The splendour of his golf, its consistency, his unfailing sportsmanship in defeat, and an appearance that became increasingly attractive with the shedding of pounds made him an heroic figure for the watching public. This was abundantly fortunate for the Royal and Ancient. Not only was he, like Palmer before him, able to attract huge crowds but they made it fashionable, almost routine, for the majority of the world's foremost golfers to compete in the Open every year. Victory became essential to lasting stature in the game's chronicles, just as it had been in the old years of Jones and Hagen.

The Open therefore had no casting problems for its play; the principal actors were readily available. The historic old links made unique stages and with the growing interest of television there was increasing scope for revealing the drama to an enormous public. Granted these advantages, the prime concern of the Royal and Ancient was to make the championship as prosperous an undertaking as possible without transgressing the bounds of good taste. Capable management became increasingly important: to ensure a stable financial basis for the future so that rising costs could be met, to improve facilities for the public, to maintain the level of prize money at a comparable rate to that of other major events and to contribute to the benefit of golf in general. Tradition has always insisted, and long may it do so, that the Open be played on a links by the sea. This state of affairs readily permits the erection of stands at various vantage points in addition to those beside the 18th hole. The United States Golf Association is less fortunate because the majority of its Open courses are set about with trees. In Britain the first stand venture was in 1963 when accommodation for 4000 spectators was erected at

several points. The cost of these and various tents was less than £2000
but a crucial start had been made, and there were other improvements.
The caddies wore smocks so that the players could easily be identified;
closed circuit television was installed in the public tents; the scoreboard
was operated on a hole-by-hole basis and there were progress boards
about the course. All this was a promise for the future, which was to be
abundantly fulfilled, though in spite of television fees the championship
made a small loss.

Everyone was disappointed when Palmer did not return to St.
Andrews in 1964, except Tony Lema who was blessed with the services
of Palmer's caddie, 'Tip' Anderson, a local golfer intimate with all the
ways of the Old Course. Lema played beautiful, composed golf in the
face of a tremendous late challenge from Nicklaus and dispelled an
ancient myth that long experience was essential to the mastering of the
Old Course. Neither he nor Nicklaus had seen it before and they had
barely two rounds practice.

The Open the following summer was notable for Thomson's fifth
victory and the first in which he had beaten a strong American field
including Palmer, Nicklaus and Lema; and also for an increase in the
television fee which helped towards a profit on the championship. Now,
it seemed, the B.B.C. had realised that it was worth covering, and the
fee was increased again the next year at Muirfield.

Gerald Micklem was Chairman of the Committee in 1965 when it
was decided that the championship at Muirfield should be extended to
four days. The thinking was that a third day with two rounds was too
long, particularly for the host of people involved in running the event.
Also by having only one round a day more golfers could qualify for the
final stages; the whole affair could proceed at a more dignified pace and
the spectators would have more time to digest the situation after 54 holes
and be able to watch a greater number of players. The change was not
made with the particular aim of increasing the revenue from the gate
and from television but, of course, it did have that effect. Even those
who thought that 36 holes on the last day was an essential and searching
test of mental and physical endurance eventually came to agree that the
change had been for the general good.

The championship was memorable for the masterfully controlled
golf of Nicklaus who, in winning for the first time, joined Sarazen,
Hogan and Player as the only men to have won all four major championships open to a professional. Much was made of the depth of the rough,
and there were jests about hay concessions, but for once there was a

much higher premium on accuracy than length. David Thomas and Doug Sanders set a splendid pace for Nicklaus who needed all his resources at the end to win by one stroke.

In spite of fine weather in 1967 and many of the world's finest golfers playing the historic links at Hoylake, the total attendance for the week was appreciably lower than those of the previous four years. The last day's crowd at Lytham in 1979 was greater than that for the whole week at Hoylake, and yet that Open made an enduring memory for all who watched.

Few golfers have inspired greater affection than Roberto De Vicenzo, the most enduring of all South American players, not only for the skill and effortless power of his golf but for rare personal qualities. His innate gentleness, faultless manners and graceful acceptance of disappointment endeared him to everyone. Frequently, for some twenty years, he had striven to win the Open and often was in close contention but not until Hoylake did his dream become reality.

After a long tense afternoon, during which he resisted, notably, the challenge of Nicklaus and Player, De Vicenzo strode down the last fairway his victory assured and the look of an emperor about him. The prolonged warmth of the applause, born of delight and relief that a great golfing person had at last been rewarded, had rarely been approached. It was an emotional moment but not one to sway the judgement of the Championship Committee that Hoylake, through no failing of the club or the links, was hardly suitable for a modern Open, although admirable for amateur occasions.

In his acceptance speech De Vicenzo said he hoped that a young British player would succeed him as champion. Few believed how soon his wish would come true. Although Player survived a memorable struggle with Nicklaus the next summer at Carnoustie, Jacklin's hour was at hand. The sight of his last drive flying far and true down the 18th fairway at Lytham always a forbidding prospect from the tee, was a deathless moment in modern Open history, a masterful gesture of confidence and control. The thunderous acclaim that greeted his jaunty figure as he moved towards his triumph was one of joy, admiration and pride that a British golfer, at least momentarily, had stemmed the tide of overseas supremacy. Eighteen years had passed since Max Faulkner had won at Portrush.

Meanwhile (in small dark rooms, so to speak), a great deal of work had been done to improve the service to spectators, not least in the provision of scoreboards and speed of information to them. Maurice

Heaney, a member of the Royal Lytham and St. Annes Club, was one of the pioneers of a system that soon was to become the envy of the United States Golf Association and other governing bodies. By now the Open had become a production that few other sports could match and that, in spite of all its beauty, the Masters at Augusta did not surpass. The Open was theatre of a high order, embracing as it often did, all the elements of drama; triumph and tragedy which often march together, joy and pathos, suspense that could be agony for the watchers, and a rare pitch of excitement when the destiny of the championship was un-resolved until the last moment of the final act. Supreme achievement in golf is a matter of heart, mind and nerve. The difference between lasting fame and oblivion rests on them and frequently the margin between the two is minute. This has been true of countless championships since the dawn of the Open, and thousands have rejoiced or suffered in the watch-ing, but since the last hole was converted into a huge amphitheatre, seating 7000 or more the dramatic effect has been much greater.

Rarely have the fractions that can turn impending glory into lasting grief been as vividly revealed as at St. Andrews in 1970. The failure of Sanders to hole from a yard for victory had no parallel in modern Open golf. Nor has any golfer been more fortunate than Nicklaus in having a second chance when defeat seemed inevitable. For Sanders the last hole was nightmare, no less. That a golfer of his experience should be unable, after a solid drive, to make a four on a hole of 360 yards without hazards of any kind, defied imagining. It served to show the relentless subtlety of the Old Course. Understandably anxious for his pitch not to finish in the Valley of Sin he overhit, was short with his first putt which looked more downhill than it was and misread the left to right break on the next one. The scene will be etched forever in the minds of the thousands watching from windows, balconies and rooftops, and clustered around Tom Morris's green, all hushed in pity for Sanders.

Twenty-four hours later Nicklaus peeled off a sweater on the 18th tee, an unwittingly theatrical gesture, and unleashed an enormous drive which raced through the green into clinging grass. Sanders, four strokes behind after thirteen holes had bravely regained three. He played a perfect run-up to four feet. Nicklaus squeezed his ball out of the rough to six feet; his putt on the same line as Sanders' the previous evening just held the break. As it fell Nicklaus hurled his putter high in the air and Sanders had to take evading action. Nicklaus was so moved that he had difficulty in paying his tributes after receiving the Cup from William Whitelaw, the Captain of the Club. Victory at St. Andrews was a cherished ambition, not only because Bobby Jones, probably his one hero in golf, had also left an indelible mark on the place.

The championship was further memorable because at its outset Jacklin held both the United States and British titles, a unique honour for a British golfer, even though the privilege lasted but a few weeks. He began his defence on the Old Course by playing thirteen holes in eight under par, then a vicious storm, which caused play to be stopped and continued the next day, interupted what might have been a record round. The prize money that year was £40,000; when the Open returned to St. Andrews eight years later it was more than three times as much. The whims of fortune played no small part in the Open at Muirfield two years later. On the 71st tee Jacklin and Lee Trevino, playing together, were level and needed two pars to beat Nicklaus. No-one who was there or watched from afar would ever forget the play at the 17th hole, as startling a turn of fortune as even the longest memory could recall. After two solid woods Jacklin was perfectly placed for a possible four or, seemingly, a five at worst. After four shots Trevino was on the back fringe of the green and for all the world looked a beaten man. He struck his chip as if heedless of the outcome but it fell into the hole. Jacklin, who had chipped short, then took three putts and was one behind. Trevino, whose moods can change within a micro-second, was transformed; he hit two flawless strokes to the 18th and shattered by a single stroke the dream of Nicklaus who, having won the Masters and U.S. Open that year, was striving for the professional Grand Slam.

There can be no telling what lasting effect that cruel reverse had upon Jacklin, not only at Muirfield but in the years that followed. He made a sadly forlorn figure as he took five on the last hole that day. Few golfers in an Open have suffered as harshly at the hands of a companion as he did during the final two rounds. In the third Trevino had holed a long putt on the 15th, an outrageously lucky bunker shot, which would have soared over the 16th green had it not hit the pin hard, and a chip from behind the last green. The chip on the 17th was, in Trevino's words, the straw that broke the camel's back. When destiny decrees that a mercurial genius such as Trevino should be blessed with continuing fortune, the dice seem irrevocably cast. That he made the most of it was a mark of his greatness.

In the spring of 1974 the Royal and Ancient decided to end the investigation, which had lasted six years, into the possibility of producing a uniform ball for the whole world. This is discussed elsewhere but the Championship Committee did decide that the 1.68 ball would be compulsory for the Open at Lytham that year. The following November its use was confirmed for all future Opens.

The 1975 Open at Carnoustie, which gave Tom Watson his first victory after a play-off with Jack Newton of Australia, showed an unexpected financial loss. This was disturbing, especially as broadcasting fees had been increased by £20,000 and the prize money had not been raised, but it proved to be only a temporary recession. Invariably during this period the Lancashire coast was a profitable setting. The crowds at Birkdale the following year were substantially larger; the broadcasting fees were raised by another £50,000 and the Open was moving into a realm of prosperity undreamed of a few years earlier. Johnny Miller won the championship in commanding fashion by six strokes; sharing second place with Nicklaus was Severiano Ballesteros, the most remarkable young talent to appear since Nicklaus himself was of a like age. At 19 the power and attack of his golf, and his strikingly handsome appearance, meant that another star had joined the cast of the Open. Not since Flory Van Donck appeared in the fifties had a golfer from the Continent of Europe made any notable impact on the championship. Ballesteros added greatly to the strength of the Open as an international event, and this strength was to mount in the years ahead.

The prelude to the 1976 championship was curiously memorable for the appearance of one, Maurice Flitcroft, which caused a deal of amusement in many quarters but not to the Championship Committee. Flitcroft, who had never played even 18 holes, decided to have a go at the Open although his only golf had been confined to hitting shots in parks and playgrounds. He sent to the Royal and Ancient for a professional entry form and gave his status as unattached, thus stealing through an unavoidable loophole in the championship conditions. A professional does not have to be a member of the Professional Golfers Association in Britain or anywhere else and there is no ready means of checking his ability and whether his entry is genuine or frivolous. Among the large numbers who enter for the qualifying rounds many are unknown and the Royal and Ancient and the United States Golf Associations agreed that checking the ability of such players would be too time consuming and might jeopardise the open nature of the championship. Amateurs, of course, have to provide confirmation that their handicap is one or better.

The evening before the first qualifying round at Formby, Flitcroft walked the course and this may have saved him strokes. His round of 121, marred by only one par, at least was consistent with halves of

61 and 60 but the fashioning of it was a decided handicap to both his partners. It was hardly surprising that they scored in the eighties and the Committee refunded their entry fees. Flitcroft seemingly was unabashed, saying he would return next year. In the event he withdrew and Nicklaus, Miller and company breathed again. Later when Flitcroft's mother was asked on the telephone why he had entered she said, 'Well, he has to start somewhere.'

Happily such frivolities have been very rare and when regional qualifying was introduced soon afterwards an adventure such as Flitcroft's would become less conspicuous. The only similar instance within memory also happened before an Open at Birkdale. An American, Walter Danecki began his challenge in 1965 with 108 at Hillside, but found Formby a sterner test and took 113. Flitcroft beat this record with some ease and if nothing else, had brought light relief to the days of waiting for the Open to begin.

For many years Turnberry had been recognised as a links worthy of an Open. Its superb setting had few, if any, peers in the British Isles but there was doubt as to its accessibility for large crowds. The condition of the links also had undergone a bad spell but eventually the Committee were satisfied that these problems could be overcome. Their decision was justified. The total crowds were the largest ever to that point in Scotland, only 5000 down on the previous record, and they were treated to the greatest and most prolonged contest between two men – Nicklaus and Watson – that the Open had ever known. Never before had two golfers, then indisputably the finest in the game, fought for the Open in such unyielding fashion, producing scores that had not previously been approached. Starting level they played the final 36 holes together, Watson in 130, ten under par, and Nicklaus a stroke more. Watson's total of 268 was eight strokes lower than the previous record, shared by Palmer and Weiskopf. The quality of their golf, in which each clearly was inspired by the other, was magnificent for its character, its attack and counter attack and the amiable spirit in which it was played. It came to an unforgettable climax when Watson, one stroke ahead, struck his final approach to two feet. Then, as anti-climax threatened, Nicklaus holed a huge putt for a three which compelled Watson to hole his for victory. It was an Open of imperishable memory.

In 1978 it seemed as if the gods had determined that the 22nd Open on the Old Course should have all the elements of success. The weather was kindly throughout, with a welcome change of wind on the last day. The crowds of 125,271 for the week exceeded the previous highest total at Lytham in 1974, by over 30,000, and Nicklaus repeated his victory of 1970. The way of it was in total contrast to the previous year when he and Watson had a private match. At St. Andrews he was pursued until the very last hole when there was a possibility that Simon Owen of New Zealand would tie. In the event Owen shared second place with Ben Crenshaw, Raymond Floyd and Tom Kite, all two strokes behind. The international aspect of the occasion was splendidly emphasised by the presence in the high places of golfers from five other countries. The most significant of these was Isao Aoki of Japan who was only a stroke off the pace after three rounds and finished seventh. His success and that of Masashi Ozaki and Tsuneyuki Nakajima, who was only seven strokes behind Nicklaus in spite of a nine at the 17th in the third round, was most timely for the Royal and Ancient.

Once again St. Andrews had provided what was, in a sense, salvation for Nicklaus. Not that he was exactly pressed for money or distinction but, as in 1970, he had not won one of the great championships for three years. The challenge of these events alone sustained his desire for competitive golf. Like Jones before him he had always been fascinated with the ever-changing problems of the Old Course and rarely in his life can he have struck so many beautifully balanced, true shots. When he walked into the last incomparable setting the massive tribute paid to him was as much for the man himself as for the supreme champion of the age. Not since James Braid in 1910 had any golfer twice been Open champion at St. Andrews. In every sense of the fitness of things it was right that Nicklaus should be next. The measure of the Royal and Ancient Club's debt to him is incalculable.

CHAPTER FOUR

THE OPEN TRANSFORMED

The upward trend in the Open's fortunes stemmed from a conversation during the championship at Hoylake in 1967. Roone Arledge of the American Broadcasting Company suggested to Wilbur M. Muirhead, Chairman of the Championship Committee, that the American Broadcasting Company and the Royal and Ancient negotiate contracts separately from those with the B.B.C. Other offers had been received from American companies but agreement with the American Broadcasting Company was reached and a large increase in fees resulted. The following year, after the Open at Carnoustie, the Club was able to cover the costs of all its championships and international match activities; to raise the prize money for 1969 and to show a healthy profit.

Thereafter all was progress. The brief policy of allowing advertising on the course, which cannot have amused members of the Honourable Company when faced with signs on the stands by the last green at Muirfield in 1966, was abandoned. As the Open continued to prosper numerous ways of exploiting it commercially were there for the taking but the Club resisted any attempts to leap on the golden chariot. One liquor firm even suggested laying bottles of its potion end to end from tee to green on a short hole as a prize for a hole-in-one.

The Club was determined not to cheapen the image of the Open or to consider sponsorship from outside. Aside from a justifiable desire for independence the risk of being obliged to rely on such sources was too great. Several events, purporting to be championships of universal significance, have appeared with fanfares of publicity and then vanished after a few years. Neither the Royal and Ancient nor the United States Golf Association have exposed themselves to the whims of commercial undertakings apart from those inescapably linked with American television. Their Open championships are the only ones of any importance not to be sponsored and thus have endured as the foremost in the world.

Television has been the major factor. Such has been the appeal of the

Open through the international strength of its entries and its growth into a great sporting occasion that contracts with the American Broadcasting Company and the B.B.C. for the coming years reveal substantial increases. Apart from these Japan and, to a lesser extent Australia, pay handsomely for the services. By 1978 no fewer than a dozen other countries were involved.

The credit for this happy state was due in great measure to Mark McCormack who, towards the end of 1977, was appointed by the Championship Committee as negotiating agent. This was a wise and profitable move. McCormack's skill and powers of persuasion in marketing his products, human or otherwise, from Arnold Palmer onwards had become legendary. Without him the Committee could never have generated such widespread interest or obtained such favourable contracts.

By revealing the drama and beauty of the Open to millions television doubtless helped to increase the number of people anxious to be there in person. In 1967 the attendance for the week at Hoylake was 29,000; six years later it had almost trebled and, although Turnberry is comparatively remote, in 1977 over 92,000 people were there during the week. The next year at St. Andrews surpassed all expectations when on each of the four days of the Open at least 23,000 watched and the total attendance exceeded 125,000.

As long ago as 1910 a golf manufacturers' exhibition marquee was erected at the Open. Its presence in succeeding years probably inspired the great spread of canvas that has since become a feature of the background to modern Opens. The marquees have been criticised as suggesting a carnival atmosphere but nothing alien to golf is allowed within. The extensions have been largely due to the demands of various companies and organisations for their own private tents with bars and television where they could entertain guests. By 1976 there were sixty such concessions, limited to seventy in 1979. Whether their presence is fitting or not they are a source of income and have the effect of reducing the number of spectators on the course.

In the early seventies the Royal and Ancient started advance sale of tickets at reduced prices if bought before January 1st or May 31st. This has proved popular to the extent that the Committee has had a substantial revenue in hand long before the championship; in May 1979 the sum was over £200,000. At the end of every Open the Secretary receives numerous requests for tickets and reserved stand seats for the following year.

An unexpected windfall, through McCormack, came the way of the Royal and Ancient in 1978. Colin Maclaine, Chairman of the Championship Committee, and Keith Mackenzie went to Japan and concluded a profitable contract with Dentsu, one of the largest advertising companies in the world. Its terms were that Dentsu would pay $50,000 annually for three years for the use of a logo representing the Open, but not the Royal and Ancient, who had the right to inspect any goods on which it was used. The Club crest was not to be shown and the logo was a likeness of the Open trophy.

Any thought that the St. Andrews attendance figures would remain records for years to come were banished at Lytham the following summer. On each of the last two days over 30,000 people were present, the first time such a total had been reached. In all 135,000 attended and even the soaring costs of some £800,000 including prize money of £155,000 and £100,000 for stands seating 17,000, were easily covered. For all the mounting prosperity the Royal and Ancient were aware of the dangers of having a 'bear by the tail'. Opportunities for commercial expansion were almost boundless but the Club were determined that the Open should not be exploited beyond the cause of the game. It was decided that the number of hospitality tents should not be increased, but what of the huge crowds? Watching on foot at Lytham was far from comfortable and would have been well nigh intolerable had poor weather prevented maximum use of the stands. However, it was thought that awareness of this among intending spectators and the breadth of the television coverage could have a restraining effect in the future.

On the threshold of the eighties the outlook for the Open was bright with promise and the victory at Lytham of Severiano Ballesteros in 1979 was symbolic. At 22 he was the youngest champion for over a century and a formidable competitor with exceptional power, flair in recovery and rare touch about the greens. These qualities, allied to attractive looks and personality, promised to make him as compelling as Arnold Palmer had been in the sixties, and his gifts had developed without any great experience in the United States. At Lytham Ballesteros beat all the leading Americans with golf of uninhibited attack and courage. At times he was fortunate in finding reasonable lies after wild drives, but he knew that the rough had been trampled by thousands of feet. His triumph, the first by a golfer from the Continent of Europe since Arnaud Massy's in 1907, denied an American victory for the sixth successive Open at Lytham.

CHAPTER FIVE

THE COMMITTEES

The General Committee

In the minds of most golfers the Royal and Ancient is associated with Rules and Championships but in common with other clubs it has the usual Committees for Handicap, Green, and House matters, as well as those for Finance, and Membership. Keeping watch over them all is the General Committee which has the final responsibility for policies and finances, with the important brief of maintaining the Club's position as a leading authority in the game. The Committee, formed in 1937 to replace the Management Committee, has eight Members, elected by the Club together with the Captain and Chairmen of the seven main Committees all of whom are *ex officio*. One of its principal functions is to decide upon major policy recommendations submitted by other Committees of the Club. At the time of writing the Chairman is W. M. Miller who in 1980 became Captain of the Honourable Company of Edinburgh Golfers, a rare link between the two most distinguished senior Clubs in the world.

The lasting strength of the Club is that there is no automatic election to it, or to its Committees, from other governing bodies. The danger that age and long service be regarded as a prime qualification and thereby gain preference over ability is thus minimised. Many young Members have served on Committees, and the Club has been fortunate in finding men with the time to give to work which is voluntary, largely anonymous and in no sense rewarding financially. The Club is no avenue for seekers after power.

The Championship Committee

Until the First World War the Open and Amateur championships were the responsibility of the clubs on whose courses they were played. Then, at a meeting in December 1919 it was suggested that the Royal and Ancient, the sole authority regarding the Rules of Golf, should assume the management of both championships, thus enhancing its position as

the game's supreme governing body. Robert Maxwell, the foremost
Scottish amateur of his time and a member of the Honourable Company,
helped to influence a decision which was in the best interests of all concerned. In February the following year W. Norman Boase, the Chairman of the Royal and Ancient Green Committee proposed that the Club
nominate a representative committee with powers to take over the duties
previously performed by the championship delegates. This was agreed
but the first Championship Committee can have had no conception of
the extent to which its duties would expand forty years later with the
growth of the Open, and the addition of other championships and international matches besides the Walker Cup.

Nonetheless it was responsible for a visionary act in 1924. At a
meeting in York, presided over by Norman Boase, Chairman of the
Committee, a Joint Advisory Committee was formed to include repre-
sentatives from the four home Unions. Its original purpose was to pre-
pare a Standard Scratch Score and Handicapping Scheme which came
into operation on March 1, 1926. In the early years there were complaints from the J.A.C. that its advice was not desired. In 1930 after
several major changes in the Rules of Golf had been considered the
J.A.C. apparently were not consulted. The J.A.C. received a cool reply
to its protest from the Chairman of the Rules, stating that his Committee
sought advice from any source it thought desirable, but saw no useful
purpose in a suggested meeting with the J.A.C. The following summer
R. C. H. Palairet, Chairman of the J.A.C. regretted that the two bodies
could not find common ground. The Secretary of the Royal and Ancient
then said that revision of the Rules was under way and that the J.A.C.'s
views would be considered but must remain confidential. This admon-
ition seemingly was ignored when notice of the changes in the Rules
was leaked to the Press.

In spite of these uneasy beginnings the J.A.C., which later became
the Council of National Golf Unions, played an important part in the
government of the game. The liaison was to prove invaluable. Norman
Boase, who had done much to make it so when there was a threatened
division between the governing bodies, died in the summer of 1938. It
was said that his 'death deprived golf in many continents of a fine states-
man'. He had travelled widely, chaired many of the Club's Committees
and, while its Captain in 1935, shared with Sir Hugh Lyon Playfair the
distinction of being Provost of St. Andrews at the same time.

The Championship Committee is composed of twelve Members of
the Club, a number increased in 1978 by the appointment of two

Business Members to advise on the mounting financial issues. Two more people, not necessarily Club Members, can be co-opted annually. The Committee is an autonomous body responsible to the General Committee only if a major financial decision, such as a large increase in the Open prize money, is involved.

After policies for the following year have been agreed at a November meeting the Chairman makes the principal decisions and bears the main responsibility for them. His election by Members of the Committee is therefore of crucial importance. Apart from being an experienced golfer he must have executive ability and be prepared to stand by decisions however unpopular they may appear to be. He will probably have to spend a hundred days or more on Royal and Ancient work every year of the three year period which is the normal term of office. This can involve loss of income, a deal of travelling and time away from home. During their terms in the seventies neither W. M. Miller nor H. C. Maclaine, his successor, was able to take annual holidays.

The demands upon the Chairman increased greatly in later years. At any time during a championship, particularly the Open, he may be faced with problems on which he has to make a final decision. These can involve anything from comparatively minor issues of staff, administration and logistics, to deciding upon the appropriate action in the event of a death threat to one of the competitors, which has happened, or whether, as at Birkdale in 1961, the Open should be postponed or abandoned in the event of continuing bad weather. Nonetheless, whatever the difficulties that may arise and the sacrifices involved in the job most contemporary Chairmen have found that they are outweighed by the satisfaction and rewards of office. They have seen the Open expand far beyond the vision of their predecessors who had to struggle with minimal budgets and usually face a loss on the championship.

Although a profit had been made on the 1950 Open the Committee was advised to seek courses in more populated areas, even inland. Fortunately the idea was rejected, possibly on traditional grounds, and as events were to prove the seaside links were the most suitable for the accommodation of large crowds and of the paraphernalia of a modern Open.

In 1952 the Touring Team Fund was insufficient to meet the cost of sending a team to the United States for the Walker Cup match the following summer. An appeal was launched and eventually produced over £2000 but A. A. Duncan, who captained the side, was advised of the need for economy.

Before television really came into the reckoning the Open income depended on gate money, car parks, entry fees and the sale of programmes. There were no ancillary sources. In 1959, when the fees from broadcasting were less than £500, the total income was only £10,000 and the championship made a loss of £1000.

If not exactly treading on eggshells the Championship Committee had to move warily from year to year. Their paramount concern was to make sufficient profit to cover expenses, increase prize money if possible and maintain a reserve fund in the event of a poor financial year resulting from strikes or continuous bad weather. Happily these contingencies have not yet arisen but there is no guarantee that one or other will not do so.

Once the Open began to prosper the Royal and Ancient were able to pursue a policy of serving the game as a whole by means of the championship's profits. In 1978 substantial sums were given to the St. Andrews Links Trust and the Professional Golfers Association; the four home Unions were absolved of their subscriptions towards the cost of international matches; the Golf Development Council and the Sports Turf Research Institute also received donations. As the future held promise of further profits a special Sub-Committee was formed to examine the many ways in which these might be ploughed back into golf. In spite of inflation the Committee also has tried to keep costs to the public as low as possible. There was no rise in admission charges for the 1979 Open. And, as far as its domestic affairs were concerned, the Club have never profited financially. No spectator at an Open need feel that his entrance fee will make any contribution towards the comfort of the Members.

From 1968 onwards the system of championship accounts was changed. Fees from broadcasting were included in what became an External Activities account because the contracts included the rights to cover events other than the Open, such as the Walker Cup or Amateur Championship. This was fair. Previously the Open account had been separate and the Club, with aid from the home Unions and smaller sources, had to bear the costs of all the other championships and matches under its control. As amateur golf was the breeding ground for the players who helped to make the Open successful it was fitting that amateur golf should be sustained.

The Selection Committee

Since the first Walker Cup match against the United States in 1922 a Royal and Ancient Selection Committee has chosen all the amateur international teams to represent Great Britain and Ireland for contests in which the Club is concerned. For many years this task, and rarely is it enviable, involved choosing only the Walker Cup team every two years but it is a task that has increased. In 1958 the World Amateur Team Championship for the Eisenhower Trophy was launched at St. Andrews, as well as a match against the Continent of Europe for the St. Andrews Trophy.

The Committee is broadly based. Only the Chairman, who normally serves for four years, need be a Member of the Club. Since 1959 the procedure has been to have one representative from each of the four home Unions. It was felt that this would best help the cause of collaboration with the Unions, and would minimise the danger of parochial interests swaying decisions. The captain of a team, the choice of whom must be confirmed by the General Committee, is co-opted to assist the selectors. Thus far the system has proved successful. No Committee is infallible and hindsight has shown that mistakes have been made but not for want of the fullest consideration of every candidate. Since the fifties no important amateur event in Great Britain or Ireland has taken place without at least one selector being present. At the Amateur championship or Lytham Trophy it is likely that the whole Committee would attend.

Very few, if any, players during the period could claim that they had not been watched and that their overall records were not known to the Committee. The old, somewhat casual, ways of selection had gone and with them the fear that selectors might lurk behind bushes, emerging in time to see only the bad shots and then disappearing. The converse could also be true and final judgement based on false premises.

Much of the credit for the present approach was due to Raymond Oppenheimer, who became chairman in 1955, and Gerald Micklem, his immediate successor. So thoroughly did they and their henchmen follow the championships and tournaments, however remote they might be, that players of any potential, whatever their background, nationality or occupation grew accustomed to being studied, often for long periods in numerous stroke or match play events. The old accusation, occasionally aired, that a man's school or university could influence selection was banished. The attitude of the selectors to the players invariably was friendly and encouraging. Oppenheimer would tell them that he was interested only in their good golf, and not the bad. Another selector of the time Tony Duncan would insist on watching a player for at least nine holes, and on one occasion did so for six different golfers within a day, so conscientious was his observation of every facet of the golf.

HELL BUNKER

THE CLUB TROPHIES

CHAPTER SIX

THE AMATEUR CHAMPIONSHIP

The Amateur championship, the senior event of its kind in the world, was the centre-piece for amateur golf long before the Royal and Ancient became the sole guide for its destiny. It was inspired by Thomas Owen Potter, the Honorary Secretary of the Royal Liverpool Club, who suggested that a tournament, open to all amateur golfers, should be held during the spring meeting at Hoylake in 1885. The Club agreed and contributed twenty-five guineas towards the purchase of a prize.

Although most of the leading players competed the tournament did not have official blessing as a championship. It was won by Allan Fullerton Macfie, an accomplished Scottish golfer who lived to be a Member of the Royal and Ancient for sixty-one years. He was not quite of the company of the great men of the time, John Ball, John Laidlay, Horace Hutchinson and others, but events conspired towards his victory. Both players in halved matches went into the next round, also it had not been arranged that all byes be accounted for in the first round, omissions which were remedied the following year, but Macfie found himself with a bye in the semi-final. While he was taking his ease Hutchinson was winning a hard match against Ball on the last green. Reaction and weariness told in the final and Macfie became the first Amateur champion, but was not confirmed as such until the Royal and Ancient took over the championship. Thus, in Bernard Darwin's words, he was retrospectively canonised.

Early the next year in 1886 B. Hall Blyth, the Captain of Royal Liverpool, suggested that the Royal and Ancient develop a real championship involving all the prominent clubs who would contribute towards a permanent trophy. The event was to be held in rotation at St. Andrews, Prestwick and Hoylake. Twenty-four clubs joined the project and each had a delegate to vote on the Committee. Hutchinson did not have to wait long for his consolation. In the final at St. Andrews in 1886 he beat H. A. Lamb by 7 and 6 over 18 holes and when the championship returned to Hoylake the following year defended it successfully.

Again he beat Ball, the Hoylake master, on the last green but Ball's turn was coming with a vengeance. He was champion eight times, and in 1890 won the Open as well as the Amateur, the only golfer ever to do so in the same year apart from Jones in 1930. Harold Hilton, the other great Hoylake golfer, won the Amateur four times and the Open twice and in 1892 would have matched Ball's feat had Ball himself not beaten him in the Amateur final at Sandwich. The influence of these two remarkable players lasted for a quarter of a century, an epoch which might be described as the golden era of amateur golf.

Royal St. George's had been added to the list of championship courses in 1892 when the Open was first played at Muirfield, only a year after the Honourable Company of Edinburgh Golfers had moved down the Forth from the links at Musselburgh. Sandwich and Muirfield, together with the three original courses, were the settings for the Amateur until, through the influence of Hutchinson, its most distinguished member, Royal North Devon at Westward Ho! was included in 1912. Hutchinson, tongue in cheek, had the nerve on behalf of the Club to point out 'how very central was its situation and how easy of approach from all directions'. The very reverse was one reason why the Amateur was only played there twice thereafter, the last time in 1931, but on this occasion Horace prevailed. The championship in 1912 was memorable for John Ball's last victory. After several perilous escapes he met Abe Mitchell of the Canteloupe Club at Ashdown Forest, the first artisan golfer to play for England, and won the final at the 38th on a wet and wild afternoon, a wonderful achievement by a man of fifty.

When the Royal and Ancient assumed control of the Open and the Amateur championships soon after the First World War a generation of great amateurs had almost gone from the reckoning. The passing years had taken toll of the golf of Ball and Hilton, who had dominated the scene for a quarter of a century; and Robert Maxwell, James Robb, James Jenkins, the champion in 1914, and others of able but lesser stature. It was time to look towards youth, and youth was nobly expressed in the persons of Cyril Tolley and Roger Wethered. Both have their places in this chronicle as Captains of the Club, but another golfer, Sir Ernest Holderness, was of their company. Holderness had preceded Tolley and Wethered at Oxford University by some years and was at his prime when the War ended. On his way to winning the championship at Prestwick in 1922 he had several close matches. In the semi-final he was fortunate that W. I. Hunter missed a short putt to win the 15th, stymied himself in doing so and was all square instead of two up. Holderness won the next two holes and beat John Caven on the last green of the final. Hunter had won the previous year at Hoylake where, in the semi-final, he beat Bernard Darwin who 'ran out of ammunition' by going out of bounds at the 19th. Had he not turned professional and gone to the United States Hunter would have remained in the forefront of British amateurs.

The return of the championship to St. Andrews in 1924 brought Holderness a second victory. His accuracy through the green, allied to a cool detachment and rare concentration when playing, became legendary. He was neither as powerful nor as spectacular as Tolley or Wethered but was equally effective in his fashion. His impact on the game would probably have lasted longer had he not risen to a high post in the Civil Service.

Of Wethered it was said that had his driving been more consistent his achievements would have been the greater but it was controlled enough at Deal in 1923. So much so, that he won the championship and, as Darwin recalled, surprised his sister into remarking, 'Why this is a new Roger'. She had travelled to Deal overnight from Burnham where she had lost in the semi-final of the British, her earliest departure from any national championship.

Every alternate year about this time the championship fell to a Member of the Club. Robert Harris, who admitted that Wethered had outplayed him at Deal, made no bones in 1925 about winning at West-ward Ho! where he disposed of his last opponent by 13 and 12. Harris then was forty-three and had reached the semi-final as far back as 1907. He played no small part in the Club's affairs. In 1922 he captained the team for the first Walker Cup match and led it on two other occasions. In the late thirties he was a prime mover in the attempt to limit the number of clubs to fourteen, and to reduce the power of the ball.

The championship at Muirfield in 1926 was memorable for the first victory by an American born golfer, Jesse Sweetser, and for a second sight of Bobby Jones. National pride probably overcame disappointment at Jones defeat in the last eight when a young Scot, Andrew Jamieson, was unafraid of what he was about and beat Jones 4 and 3. Soon after-wards at Lytham, Jones took the first step towards becoming the first man to win the Open championships of Britain and the United States in the same year, but Jamieson's performance took its place in history as the last man to beat Jones in any British championship.

The name of William Tweddell became as famous in defeat as in victory. Although he won the Amateur impressively at Hoylake in 1927 it was his refusal to yield to Lawson Little until the last green at Lytham eight years later that stirred the admiration of golfers everywhere. Little, many years Tweddell's junior, was immensely powerful. The previous summer at Prestwick he had produced some of the most lethal golf ever played in the championship and had destroyed James Wallace by 14 and 13. He then won the United States championship, a double he repeated in 1935 but not before Tweddell had made him work desperately hard. At one point in the morning Tweddell was five down but Little could not get clean away from him. After twenty-six holes he was three up but Tweddell squared the match, and when two up on the 35th tee Little lost the hole to a beautiful bunker shot. On the last green Tweddell's putt of some six yards to prolong the match just failed.

In the meantime Philip Perkins had confirmed his stolid competitive ability by beating Wethered in the final at Prestwick. In the last eight Wethered had been given a rare fright by J. B. Pease, later Lord Wardington, who took him to the 21st. Pease, who was fifty-nine, had been one up on the 18th tee. An even more remarkable instance of mature skill and patience overcoming age and a long ordeal was the victory of the Hon. Michael Scott at Hoylake in 1933. At fifty-four he became the oldest of all the Amateur champions. Day after day he quietly kept the ball in play and allowed his opponents to make the mistakes.

The same was partly true of Tolley who, at a like age, made Frank Stranahan play solid golf to beat him in the semi-final at St. Andrews in 1950. The memory of Tolley, pipe in mouth, strolling contentedly round the Old Course, caddie bearing his clubs in a light bag, is still clear. He swung the club with a measured ease and power, confounding the thought that thirty years had passed since he first won the championship. Joe Carr, his victim on the morning of the Stranahan match, was not then born. All this made for watching as memorable as the slow final between Stranahan and Richard Chapman was forgettable.

Joe Carr, with his remarkable flair and engaging personality, and who, for all his huge length, could not overcome Tolley, was becoming the great axe of a formidable quartet of Irish golfers; himself, Cecil Ewing, James Bruen and Max McCready. For a while after the Second World War they alone stemmed a series of American victories. Two of the finest British Amateurs of the pre-war period, Jack McLean and Hector Thomson, had turned professional but not before Thomson had beaten James Ferrier, an Australian, on the last green of the Old Course in 1936. Two years later the vast figure of Ewing had lost the final to the imperishable Charles Yates of Atlanta and Augusta fame. After the War, eyes looked towards a new generation, and Bruen immediately gave the lead when he out-gunned Robert Sweeny, one of the most graceful of golfers.

McCready, whose golf had elements of majesty, whose confidence seemed boundless, won a great match from behind against William Turnesa, one of the finest American short game players of the age. That was at Portmarnock in 1949, the only time the championship had ever been held outside Britain. The Irish Golf Union represented the whole country and politics then were not allowed to interfere with sport. The South African problem was far away.

Since 1896 when the final was extended from 18 to 36 holes the organising clubs, and subsequently the Royal and Ancient, had seen no cause to alter the form of the championship. Then, in 1955 N. C. Selway and his Championship Committee decided that at Troon the next year the quarter and semi-finals also should be played over 36 holes. This reactionary step stemmed from a desire to help the preparation of international teams. The British had suffered its heaviest defeat on home ground in the 1955 Walker Cup match at St. Andrews. David Blair and Ian Caldwell alone won points. It was thought that a fresh and more thorough approach to the selection of future teams was essential and Raymond Oppenheimer was appointed Chairman of a new committee. As the Walker Cup matches then were over 36 holes, a distance of which few had any experience, it seemed possible that this could be gained from the late rounds in the championships.

The plan met considerable criticism, from those who claimed that the game was one of 18 holes; that the championship should not be used as a Walker Cup trial; that the watching value for spectators could be reduced with only four matches on the fourth day and two on the fifth; and that the 36 hole match tended to eliminate the element of uncertainty which many considered to be part of the charm of match play. Furthermore the field had to be reduced and this involved balloting which was not popular. The Committee were undeterred but, in their wildest flight of fancy, neither they nor anyone else could have foreseen the outcome of the championship at Troon. Its form seemed a positive guarantee against the unexpected happening, but happen it did with the victory of John Beharrell. He was just eighteen, the youngest of all Amateur champions, and by curious coincidence the first English champion since Michael Scott, who was the oldest.

There was no small irony in the success of such an inexperienced competitor, but neither was there any fortune to it. In successive rounds he beat Charles Lawrie, Ian Caldwell, Gene Andrews, a most able American, and, over 36 holes, Frank Deighton, Reid Jack, probably the best British amateur of the period, and lastly Leslie Taylor. So consistently did Beharrell keep the ball in play and so remarkable was his touch around and on the greens that, even to experienced observers, his progress seemed inevitable. At his first attempt he had achieved what many fine golfers had failed to do after years of striving. It was a week of dreams for a young man and one of the most extraordinary championships of all.

The same 36 hole formula was used the following year at Formby, where Jack justly came into his own by beating an American, Harold B. Ridgley, in the final, but changes were made for the 1958 championship on the Old Course. In order to reduce a huge entry to the workable figure of 200, regional qualifying, 36 holes stroke play, was introduced. Thereby it was hoped that many more players would be attracted to enter, but this was not so and the practice was soon abandoned.

There had been so many instances of good players clashing in early rounds that, for the first time, it was decided to seed the draw. Sixteen players thus were favoured, a number that later was reduced to eight. Also only the semi-finals and final were played over 36 holes. A most successful championship came to a fitting climax with victory for Carr, the most formidable match player in the islands, who beat Alan Thirlwell, whose golf had few peers for its natural ease and power. In his quarter final Thirlwell holed a longish putt on the last green to beat Bob Charles, who had putted dead from the Valley of Sin. Five years later Charles was Open champion.

Further to the cause of examining the leading amateurs over 36 holes the Championship Committee had arranged for an annual match against a professional team. It produced several entertaining contests, not least at Turnberry in 1958 when Gerald Micklem's team beat what was, with one exception, the victorious Ryder Cup side of the previous year. This stirred lively optimism, falsely as it proved, for the Walker Cup match the following summer at Muirfield. The selectors chose what seemed the strongest team but it proved sadly vulnerable in starting and in finishing several matches. Mighty American youth, in the persons of Nicklaus and his young friends, was an unexpected factor. All four foursomes were lost, and the final outcome a harsh disappointment after hopes had been so high.

The 36 hole semi-finals were retained for the next two occasions at

Sandwich and Portrush but in 1961 the championship reverted to its traditional form. If the 36 hole experiment had proved little it had shown a willingness by the Royal and Ancient to make changes if the reasons appeared to be valid, and to abandon them if they were not. As it happened the Walker Cup match in Seattle that year was the last to be played over 36 holes. The crushing defeat by 11–1 showed that experience of the longer matches was not a significant factor in the strengthening of British teams. Martin Christmas won the only point for Great Britain.

When the championship returned to St. Andrews two years later Michael Lunt made his mark on its history. His victory was the first by a British golfer in the year of a visiting American Walker Cup team since Wethered won in 1923. In his semi-final Lunt beat an admirable golfer in Ed Updegraff who in 1975 captained a winning United States team on the Old Course. On the 16th tee Lunt was three up, but Updegraff won the next two holes in superb fashion and finally, as a cold grey haar swept up the last fairway Lunt had to hole from six feet for the match. In the final Lunt faced John Blackwell, a blithe spirit and an ardent worshipper of the Old Course whose greatest ambition was to excel in a championship there. He was apprehensive of playing a man some twenty years his junior and a much more powerful golfer but he need not have feared. A splendid match lasted for 35 holes and Blackwell had lost with honour. In 1966 he was elected Captain of the Club, three years after his brother, Thomas.

Lunt, whose father was an English Champion, was one of the small company to have won the British and English championships. He also lost a final in each of them, one to Gordon Clark at the 39th when defending his British title, the other to Michael Bonallack whose era had been launched in 1961 when the Amateur was played for the first time at Turnberry. Not until the morning of the final against James Walker did he have to play the last two holes.

No golfer since the great years of John Ball dominated British amateur golf to the extent that Bonallack did throughout the sixties. He won the English and Amateur championships five times each and a host of other first class events. His last three victories in the Amateur were successive, and he was the only golfer to have won it in all four home countries. After Turnberry it was written that 'Bonallack's victory was the fulfilment of many qualities; a remarkable devotion to the game, boundless perseverence and quiet determination, self control and poise at all times and a rare modesty. No golfer has accepted disappointment or triumph more gracefully.' Nothing that happened thereafter altered this estimate of an exceptional character and in golfing terms it was soon clear that he was one of the greatest of championship competitors. He had the precious gift of being able to raise his game against a strong opponent, and even when, as sometimes happened, his swing was awry he held his game together with golf around the greens and putting that for ten years had no equal in Britain. If Bonallack's record in Walker Cup matches was not as impressive as he would have wished it was partly because of his concern for the team's success rather than his own. This, and the knowledge that much was expected of him, occasionally proved too heavy a burden but his greatest ambition was realised when he led his side to the famous victory at St. Andrews.

Throughout his career Bonallack was a symbol of the finest that amateur golf can produce. It was characteristic of his nature that he should serve the Royal and Ancient, and the game which had given him so much, and in many ways other than in the playing of it. In time he served on the Implements and Ball Committee, and as Chairman of the Amateur Status and Selection Committees.

When the championship returned to the Old Course after an interval of thirteen years Richard Siderowf of the United States regained the title he had won in 1973 at Porthcawl, but not without the aid of fortune. On his way to the final he survived several tight matches mainly because his opponents made serious errors on the closing holes, but Siderowf was an unyielding competitor. No matter how desperate the situation might be, his handsome features revealed no sign of emotion, the rhythm of his swing no trace of haste. An indication of this was his stroke to the 17th green in the afternoon of the final when he was one down to John Davies. He squared the match there and won it when Davies took three putts on the 37th. This was a great disappointment for British followers because Davies had been the outstanding golfer of the week. Siderowf, a stockbroker by profession and an amateur in the full sense of the term, joined Little and Stranahan as the only Americans to have won the championship twice.

In the meantime Trevor Homer, from the Midlands of England, had won a surprising victory at Sandwich which he repeated two years later at Muirfield when he beat James Gabrielson of the United States in the final. Homer then turned professional but, as others had done before him, discovered the considerable difference that lies between winning matches and competing for money at stroke play. Year after year the potential rewards of professional tournament golf attracted some of the most gifted young players; then, at the very time when the British amateur game was in need of an outstanding figure, Peter McEvoy won the championship at Ganton in 1977. He defended it successfully the following year at Troon, only the fifth golfer to do so in the history of the event.

After the Second World War the championship became an increasing attraction for American golfers of diverse ages and talent, to such an extent that they sometimes filled a fifth or more of the places in the draw. Weight of numbers, however, was not always revealed in quality of performance. In 1978 not one of the huge American entry reached the last eight and very few survived the early rounds. The Championship Committee felt that further evidence of ability than a handicap was essential if the standard of the event were to be preserved. The United States Golf Association agreed that from 1979 onwards entries would only be accepted from golfers who had qualified for either a United States Open or Amateur championship during the previous five years. This had a salutary effect on the field at Hillside where only twenty-seven Americans were in the draw. The closing rounds on this occasion had a pleasingly international flavour and the two strongest members of the victorious American Walker Cup team reached the final, in which Jay Sigel, a golfer of enduring amateur status with a beautiful, measured style, beat Scott Hoch, a young college player. For the first time in the championship's history not a single British or Irish golfer reached the semi-finals but, by narrowly failing to do so, an Indian, Lakshman Singh, progressed much further than any of his countrymen had ever done before.

For generations the championship has served a splendid purpose and has produced much memorable golf but it has not been a profitable venture for the Royal and Ancient. When it was first played on the Old Course in 1886 the Club had a credit of £27 which was spent on prizes. Ninety years later at St. Andrews the deficit was some £3400, and in 1978 this deficit had risen to over £7500. The reason for the apparently heavy expense is the Club's determination to ensure that, within their context, the facilities do not fail by comparison with those for the Open. These do not involve stands, a major expense, but include the erection of scoreboards, press arrangements, circulation of draw sheets and programmes, the presence of Club officials and Committee Members, and preparation of the course.

In 1949 the Royal and Ancient took over the Boys championship, which was founded by Thomas South and Donald Mathieson in 1921, and in 1963 accepted responsibility for the Youths. Both these events involve considerable expense, particularly as they are preceded by international matches, but their value to the game cannot be measured in cost. Countless boys under eighteen and youths under twenty-two have gained experience from them, and many have reached the game's highest levels. The Seniors championship for golfers who have lived for at least fifty-five years was started in 1969, but is only a two-day event and its cost generally is covered by the entry fees.

The financial outlay essential to the efficient organisation of all these championships for amateurs reflects the policy of using profits from the Open for the benefit of the game as a whole. And amateur golfers are much the greater part of it.

CHAPTER SEVEN

THE WALKER CUP –
The Great Crusade

The first international match between Britain and the United States was played at Hoylake in 1921, and if the home side began by feeling complacent about the outcome they soon learned otherwise. The American team, which included Bobby Jones, Francis Ouimet and Charles Evans, won all four foursomes and five of the eight singles. Cyril Tolley beat Evans, and Tommy Armour, who was to become one of the greatest of professional golfers when he went to the United States, won his match for Britain. Otherwise there was little consolation for Britain; the shape of events to come had been determined.

The previous year G. H. Walker, as President of the United States Golf Association had been involved in a conference on the Rules with the Royal and Ancient. He was inspired with the thought of an international match not least because he had been educated partly at Stonyhurst School and had many ties with England. At first it was thought that several countries might be included in the event but finally, and happily, it became and remained a private contest between Great Britain & Ireland, and the United States. Since the first official match in 1922 at the National Links on Long Island it has been a kind of sacred crusade for British and Irish golfers, who have pursued it with deathless enthusiasm and no great success. Of the twenty-seven matches two have been won and one halved. Occasionally the margin of defeat has been overwhelming, particularly in the United States, but there has never been any suggestion by either side that the contest be abandoned or that British teams should be strengthened by the inclusion of golfers from other countries.

After the worst defeat since the Second War, at Seattle in 1961, Joe Dey, then Executive Director of the United States Golf Association, was asked whether there was danger of the Americans tiring of what frequently was a one-sided contest. He replied that their only concern was whether the British might wish to end the match. From the beginning it was clear that Britain could not possibly match certain blessings enjoyed by the United States such as numbers of accomplished players and greater opportunities of competitive play in good conditions. This was particularly true of college golfers but feeling on this score has waned since British sides have also included players who could be described as full-time amateurs waiting to turn professional. The lasting significance of the Walker Cup is that it has been a symbol of the golfing friendship between the two nations. For the majority of golfers, playing in a Walker Cup match is the summit of achievement as an amateur, surpassing for some the winning of a national championship. No sporting contest between countries has been played with greater harmony, in greater earnest, or in a finer spirit.

Aside from the responsibility of the Royal and Ancient for choosing teams, and organising the match every fourth year when it is in Britain, the history of the affair is closely associated with St. Andrews. The Old Course was the setting for the triumphs in 1938 and 1971, and six other matches have been played there. In the first two of these, in 1923 and 1926, the Americans might well have been beaten (words that were often echoed down the years), but for their resilience on the brink of failure. Three of the foursomes were won, but one single turned the whole contest head over heels. W. W. Mackenzie, six-up after fourteen holes, lost twelve of the next eighteen to brilliant golf by G. V. Rotan. An apparently certain point for Britain had gone. Ouimet, two down and three to play against Wethered, finished 3–4–3 and squared his match, and F. J. Wright who was in the same plight against Ernest Holderness, won the last three holes.

The remarkable American recovery was not surpassed until 1965 when they won six and halved one of the last eight singles and saved the match at Baltimore. At the end it was the British who were seeking salvation from an awful collapse. Clive Clark was two down and three to play in the last match but in one of the bravest of recoveries finished all square, holing a long putt on the 18th green. Again on the Old Course in 1926 the United States won by a single point. Wethered, who frequently gave his side an inspiring lead, won the first foursome with Holderness. The other three were lost but Wethered, Harris, the British Captain, Eustace Storey and Jamieson won their singles and Charles Hezlet halved.

Thus far the Walker Cup had provided some stirring golf and absorbing finishes but dark times were ahead, so dark that Bernard

Darwin, writing in 1944, was moved to describe the series as calamitous for Britain, and that but for the victory in 1938 he could hardly have borne to write about it. His passionate spirit must have been sorely troubled and with good reason. After 1926 the next five contests were lost by enormous margins. Of the sixty matches played the British could only win six. On three occasions the name of Tony Torrance and once that of Leonard Crawley alone saved the scoresheet from an unbroken series of British noughts. This was humiliating and it was feared that the Americans might well become bored with repeated unchallenged success. There were lively murmurs of protest that the Championship Committee, responsible for choosing the teams, were not sufficiently qualified for the task. The murmurs grew stronger as the General Meeting in 1936 approached. Sir John Simon, as Captain, was in control of the Meeting and anger was stemmed only when it was announced that an entirely new Selection Committee would be formed.

In making a fresh start the Committee chose J. B. Beck, a shrewd, cheerful, positive personality, as captain. In the search for players the net was cast wider than had been customary and it was decided to have a trial match at St. Andrews about the time of the Spring Meeting. This helped to unite people from various parts of the country and from varying backgrounds. In those days there were not so many competitions as in the years ahead and players did not have the same opportunity of knowing each other. It happened that most of the players at the trial acquitted themselves well and then it fell to Beck to bring forth the finest from the chosen team. He did so in splendid fashion but if he were a considerable force behind the scenes the golf of James Bruen, who was just 18, was a tremendous inspiration. So commanding was his play in practice before the match that he attracted more attention than did the Americans. It was felt that no matter how good were the visitors they could not play better than Bruen, who was constantly scoring in the sixties. This impression spread through the side of which every member contributed to the victory.

Bruen and Harry Bentley halved the leading foursome. Crawley and Frank Pennink, and Gordon Peters and Hector Thomson won theirs. Although Bruen lost his single to Yates, winner of the Amateur championship a few days earlier, and one of the most appealing figures in American golf for years to come, his influence had done its invaluable work. Peters and Thomson won commandingly, Charles Stowe narrowly and as Cecil Ewing was about to win on the last green Alec Kyle was walking triumphantly home. The deed was done by seven matches to four and the tide of failure stemmed, but long years were to pass before the Old Course saw such scenes of joy again.

The first eight post-war matches followed a pattern. The United States were not sorely pressed in their own land and although there were times in Britain when optimism foresaw a closer result than actually happened a British victory was not a lively prospect until 1963. After the debacle at Seattle it had been decided to play the matches over 18 holes with sets of foursomes and singles on each of the two days. Great was the rejoicing the first evening at Turnberry when the British and Irish, having restricted the Americans to only one win in the singles actually led by three points. Surely victory was in sight, but anxiety in the face of American resolve was largely responsible for a disastrous second day when only David Sheahan of Ireland and Ronnie Shade won, but braver times were coming.

Next came the halved match in Baltimore and then again the Old Course was the scene of a famous victory at precisely the moment when it was needed. For the first time the British won all four foursomes but promptly felt the recoil and when, at lunch on the second day, the United States led by two points with eight singles to play high expectations had become wishful thinking for most of the home side's supporters. In the first match Michael Bonallack fell to withering golf from Lanny Wadkins and in the last Geoffrey Marks was to lose to Tom Kite. In every other match the tale was one of unbroken success. Six went to the 17th green or beyond and if the Americans were vulnerable in most of the finishes their failure was due in no small measure to the courage and determination of the opposition. When David Marsh hit the stroke of his lifetime to the 17th green and became dormy on William Hyndman triumph was assured. Bonallack's leadership, as powerful a factor as John Beck's had been in 1938, together with shrewd team selection by Sandy Sinclair and his Committee, were the foundation of victory. Seven of the last day's twelve matches finished on the Tom Morris green and in the evening sunshine the ageless setting had never seemed more beautiful. People were massed on every hand, watching from windows, balconies and rooftops. The Old Course had known many momentous days, and others were to follow, but few stirred the heart as this one did.

Two years later, at The Country Club in Brookline, the match was desperately poised until the closing holes. Only the calmness under strain of Danny Edwards and Marty West, and the unyielding spirit of Vinnie Giles, prevented the Walker Cup from remaining in Britain. There was little sign of its being regained in 1975. One of the most powerful of all

American teams included Jerry Pate, U.S. Open champion the following summer, and several others who soon made their mark as successful professionals. Four points down after the first day left faint hope of recovery for Britain, and a foursome the next morning turned against Charles Green and Hugh Stuart who were one up and three to play. Although the home side briefly were ahead in six singles they could not stay the pace.

After three close matches in the United States the British performance in 1977 at Shinnecock Hills was disappointing. At first it seemed that the superb course would not be unfavourable to the British, but it was decidedly American in the clawing thickness of the rough and the rare swiftness of the greens. In practice the British had shown that they could play it well but in the final analysis a strong nucleus of four American college golfers, who all subsequently turned professional, won their matches mostly by greater freedom from the basic errors that beset some of the British at crucial moments. Defeat by 16–8 was the heaviest since the matches first were played over 18 holes in 1963.

If at Shinnecock there was never any lively prospect of a British victory the next engagement at Muirfield remained tautly balanced until the last hour on the final afternoon. At one point the British were fractionally ahead and a splendid finish seemed probable but anti-climax was at hand. When the strain became severe the Americans missed fewer fairways, holed more telling putts and occasional British errors contributed to the loss of seven singles. Allan Brodie alone was victorious for Britain.

As often before the decisive factor was that the Americans had emerged from a much more severe competitive background than the British. Inevitably they will continue to have this advantage but in a tediously commercial sporting age the Walker Cup match is an uncommon symbol of the spirit in which a game should be played. It is also an expression of the concord and unity of purpose which exists between the governing bodies of the two foremost golfing nations.

CHAPTER EIGHT

THE WORLD AMATEUR TEAM CHAMPIONSHIP

The heroic, when it involves supreme effort on behalf of others, is rare in championship golf. Mostly the individual is concerned with his own fate only, but occasionally, as in the World Amateur Team Championship, the responsibility is greater. When borne alone on such an occasion it can be an awesome burden demanding uncommon courage, control and technique. Ian Hutcheon, a quiet, modest man from Angus, revealed these qualities to a degree that few British golfers have matched in Portugal in 1976. His great last round at Penina enabled Britain and Ireland to win the championship for the second time, a notable achievement in modern world competition.

Although the Championship sometimes could be a laborious affair it rarely failed to produce exceptional golf or a stirring finish. The idea was conceived by the United States Golf Association and suggested to the Royal and Ancient early in 1958. A conference was held in Washington in May. Delegates from 35 nations attended and the World Amateur Golf Council was formed. It was decided that the two principal governing bodies should share control. The Chairmen of the General and Championship Committees normally represent the Club. Friends of American golf presented a trophy which President Eisenhower agreed should be named after him, and the first championship was played on the Old Course in the autumn of that year. Teams from twenty-nine countries competed.

The occasion was memorable for the last appearance at St. Andrews of Bobby Jones, who was captain of the United States team, but his farewell was not blessed with victory. The United States tied with Australia, one stroke ahead of Britain and Ireland. The Australians won the play-off over 18 holes by two strokes. It seemed incredible that with totals of over 900 strokes three teams could finish so close together, but this has happened more than once.

The Championship is decided by the aggregate of the three lowest scores in each round from the teams of four. This still makes calculation of relative positions difficult during the round when it is uncertain which player's score will eventually be discarded. Unless one has returned a hopeless score each player is burdened by not knowing whether to attack or defend, or to take a safe middle course. Mention has been made elsewhere of William Hyndman's magnificent stroke to the 17th in the last round, but a few minutes earlier Arthur Perowne, third man for Britain, hit an equally great stroke with a two iron to within six feet. Like Hyndman he holed for a three. This birdie and one at the 16th had given his side a chance of victory but thinking that another was essential Perowne putted too strongly at the last and missed the one back. Eventual defeat certainly was not his fault; his score was the lowest that day and the fault lay with others.

It was then Australia's turn to be tormented by this uncertainty. If Peter Toogood could finish with two fours the task of Hyndman and Guy Wolstenholme of Britain, the last men for their teams, would be almost impossible. Toogood's first putt at the 17th finished a yard from the hole; he missed and in attempting to tap in the ball hit it twice. This awful blunder might have cost Australia victory but neither Hyndman nor Wolstenholme was able to make a three at the 18th, the one for an American win, the other for Britain to tie. Bruce Devlin celebrated his twenty-first birthday with splendid golf throughout for Australia and, together with Reid Jack and Hyndman returned the lowest individual score.

If all was tension and doubt to the very last putt at St. Andrews the next championship at Merion in the United States in 1960 was the very reverse. The wonderful scoring of Nicklaus, then twenty, was the lowest ever returned by an amateur on an important international occasion. His total of 269 was mainly responsible for an American victory by forty-two strokes. The event was somewhat costly for Joe Carr who, rashly as it proved, wagered his scores against those of Nicklaus and lost a substantial number of dollars to him.

Great Britain and Ireland finished third, as they did in Japan two years later. They were still a long way behind the United States who won, but consolation was to follow at Olgiata, north of Rome, in 1964. The golf was beset with gusting winds and thunder rain. After a day's trampling the soft greens resembled football pitches and while making putting difficult for everyone probably made life hardest for the Americans, accustomed to fast, manicured surfaces. Even Beman, one of the great putters of the time, was troubled by them. Although Michael Bonallack was below form, Shade, Lunt and Rodney Foster all played with great resolution and returned telling scores. Great Britain and Ireland led throughout but were given an almost unbearable hour in the dripping gloom of the final afternoon before victory was certain. Their total seemed safe from challenge when Keith Alexander, the last of the Canadians, needed to play the last five holes in as many under par to tie. In a remarkably courageous effort he had four successive birdies but to the enormous relief of Joe Carr's team, missed the 18th green, Canada finished two strokes behind and for a while the Eisenhower Trophy resided in the Royal and Ancient Clubhouse.

Defence of the Trophy in Mexico in 1966 was weakened when Bonallack tore muscles in his back early in the third round. He was badly hampered but struggled on gamely because Peter Townsend had completely lost confidence. Eventually splendid golf by Shade, supported by Gordon Cosh enabled their side to finish third. In 1968 the British team failed by a stroke to tie with the United States at Royal Melbourne when Shade's putt of six feet on the last green failed to drop. Thereafter performance declined until the historic day in Portugal.

In the meantime politics had made its tiresome intrusion. In 1974 the Championship was due to be played in Kuala Lumpur but the Malaysian Government would not agree to a South African team competing there. The event was taken to the Dominican Republic who had no such objections; neither had Portugal in 1976. South Africa and Rhodesia both sent teams to Penina and thus the British triumph there was complete.

The last afternoon was unforgettable. On a long course, where wet greens became ever more treacherous John Davies, Michael Kelley, Steve Martin and Hutcheon had toiled bravely for three days and had a slight lead for their side. When Davies, third man out in the last round, finished Hutcheon was playing the 11th. The destiny of the whole affair now rested upon Hutcheon and his companions, M. Mori of Japan and Tony Gresham of Australia, the Republic of China and the United States. The little company of British followers were thankful that Hutcheon was the man. His game had always been founded on steadiness; the pace of his swing never varied and whatever the turn of events his manner was undisturbed. He had been chosen as the team's sheet anchor; in the event he produced the one great round.

The last eight holes demanded long, accurate striking but Hutcheon played them in four under par and was within a whisker of two more birdies. Against such golf the challenge about him faded, save for that of

Mori. The little Japanese fought gallantly until the end but Hutcheon, calm and impassive, yielded nothing and crowned an admirable team performance. It was a proud day for him, for British golf and for the Royal and Ancient.

CHAPTER NINE

THE RULES OF GOLF

Every year the Royal and Ancient Club receives from Unions, Associations and Clubs in all parts of the world hundreds of queries on various aspects of the Rules of Golf. The majority concern incidents arising in actual play; others require decisions on the legality of equipment, arising from the increasing ingenuity of manufacturers or amateur inventors hoping to profit from the growing market. The introduction of a velocity test for golf balls in 1976 imposed a further responsibility since Approved Lists of brands have to be published. The Club constantly reviews the Rules of the game and is frequently asked to advise countries where golf is developing. Its work never ceases.

For many years Niel Loudon, Secretary of both the Rules and the Amateur Status Committees, has been the permanent official in charge of this aspect of the Club's work. Few men are as knowledgeable on the Rules, and he is able to deal with most of the queries himself but when there is no precedent and the queries require debate on points of principle, they are circulated to Members of the appropriate Committee for their decision. From time to time the decisions are made available in loose leaf form on payment of an annual subscription. The revenues from this service, and the fees for ball testing, are the main source of income which enables the operation to function efficiently.

The Rules of Golf Committee entertains queries from official bodies only as otherwise it might be in an invidious position if it were to back an individual who was in dispute with his own Club Committee. Also the Rules Committee might find itself wasting time dealing with hypothetical queries thought up in the locker room or bar. On the other hand Amateur Status is a personal matter and every query from an individual is considered.

The principal aim of the Club, working in close collaboration with the United States Golf Association, is to make the Rules of Golf as uniform and simple as possible and to keep changes to a minimum. The vast sums of money in professional tournaments make it all the more important for the governing bodies to ensure that there are no loopholes which might make it difficult for fair decisions to be given. Local rules introduced by professional bodies must also be kept under review to ensure that the Rules of Golf are not eroded.

The Rules must be uniform and it is crucial that their interpretation should be likewise. To this end there is continuous liaison between the R. and A. and the U.S.G.A. For example in 1975 J. Stewart Lawson, elected Captain of the Club in 1979, an authority on the Rules and a former Chairman of the Committee, prepared a 'Comparative Analysis of R. and A. and U.S.G.A. Decisions'. This has proved invaluable to both governing bodies in their efforts to achieve uniformity. Every four years, at the time of the Walker Cup match in Britain, the two bodies hold their principal conference to decide what changes to recommend. During the years preceding the conference the R. and A. consults over fifty affiliated golfing nations at home and overseas, and also the P.G.A., on proposed changes and invites constructive suggestions. Before any amendments can become law and are recommended in the Code published the following January, they are submitted through the General Committee to a Business Meeting of the Club, and must receive favourable votes from not less than two-thirds of the Members present. As the Members represent numerous countries and are golfers of every standard a democratic process is preserved. This has been so since the authority of the Royal and Ancient regarding the rules became absolute in 1897, a comparatively recent date in the long chronicle of golf. The game, as an identifiable pastime, had been played in Scotland for three centuries before anyone, even Royalty, among its enthusiasts thought it necessary to introduce a code of rules. Golf then simply was an exercise in hitting a ball from one point to another. The players were not concerned with refinements of style; no-one then remarked on another's faulty weight transference, plane of swing or individual finger tension, although doubtless they suffered their frustrations. It is unlikely that James VI of Scotland, while playing on the North Inch at Perth, would send in for a ruling when his ball was in a bad lie, and await a courtier to hasten out and allow him a free drop. He would have taken it anyway.

It fell to the Honourable Company of Edinburgh Golfers, then the Company of Gentlemen Golfers, to produce the first code of rules in 1744, as a basis of conduct for the annual Silver Club competition on the links at Leith. The original thirteen articles were:

1. You must tee your ball within one club's length of the hole.

2. Your tee must be upon the ground.

3. You are not to change the ball you strike off the tee.

4. You are not to remove Stones, Bones, or any Break Club, for the sake of playing your Ball, except upon the Fair Green and that only within a Club's length of your Ball.

5. If your Ball come among watter or any wattery filth, you are at liberty to take out your Ball and bringing it behind the hazard and teeing it, you may play it with any club and allow your Adversary a stroke, for so getting out your ball.

6. If your balls be found anywhere touching one another you are to lift the first ball, till you play the last.

7. At Holing, you are to play your Ball honestly for the Hole, and not play upon your Adversary's Ball, not lying in your way to the Hole.

8. If you should lose your Ball, by its being taken up, or any other way you are to go back to the Spot, where you struck last, and drop another Ball, and allow your adversary a Stroke for the misfortune.

9. No man at Holing his Ball is to be allowed, to mark his way to a Hole with his Club or anything else.

10. If a Ball be stopp'd by any person, Horse, Dog or anything else, the Ball so stopp'd must be play'd where it lyes.

11. If you draw your Club, in order to Strike and proceed so far in the Stroke, as to be bringing down your Club: If then your Club shall break, in any way, it is to be Accounted a Stroke.

12. He whose Ball lyes farthest from the Hole is obliged to play first.

13. Neither Trench, Ditch or Dyke, made for the presentation of the Links, nor the Scholar's Holes or the Soldier's Lines, shall be accounted a Hazard. But the Ball is to be taken out and Tee'd and play'd with any Iron Club.

The articles were signed by John Rattray, an Edinburgh surgeon who, having won the Silver Club competition, was the Company's first Captain. He was again successful the following year but, as the history of the Honourable Company tells, his golf was abruptly curtailed that autumn when he was commanded to act as surgeon to the troops of Prince Charles at Prestonpans. This was possibly the first time that warfare, as so often in the following centuries, interfered with golf but doubtless the

Company continued to enjoy their claret. Rattray apparently remained with Prince Charles until the last dark act at Culloden where he was taken prisoner. The intervention of a fellow member, Duncan Forbes, Lord President of the Court of Session, who had striven to prevent the Jacobite rising, saved him from execution, and Rattray was able to compete again for the Silver Club in 1748.

The rules, which arose from the vision of Rattray and his friends, embrace the essence and spirit of the modern code but they specified no penalties for divergence from them. Allowance, with a penalty of one stroke, was made for lost ball or one in what was the forerunner of the water hazard, otherwise it was presumed that no Gentleman golfer would indulge in any underhand tricks, like nudging out of a poor lie. Such malpractice would soon have come to light among so few players, all of whom were well known to each other. Once the variables of a vast number of golfers had to be taken into account it became a different matter, but a century and more were to pass before the number of rules greatly increased. This was because they were mostly concerned with match and not stroke play.

In 1754 it was natural that the Society of St. Andrews Golfers should adopt the code for their first Silver Club competition, especially since the Gentlemen Golfers were anxious to compete at St. Andrews, and did so. The only change from the code was in Rule 5 where the player had to throw his ball behind him and not tee it as at Leith where the ground was softer.

The first specific mention of the ball being played where it lay, except in Rule 10 referring to outside agency, was in the Edinburgh code of 1775. Even as late as 1812 there was no specific Royal and Ancient rule to that effect except the one concerning a rabbit scrape from which the player must play as it from any 'common Hazard'. This surely meant any poor lie and was accepted as such until clarified later in what is now Rule 16.

The original rule regarding touching balls was partly designed to prevent any croquet type malice, but the right for one player's ball to obstruct another was retained when, in 1775, touching was defined as being within six inches. In effect this was the birth of the stymie rule, one which caused as much argument as any other until it was finally abandoned in 1952. The opponents of the stymie did have one year of relief when at the September Business meeting in 1833 a motion to abolish it was carried unanimously, but a year later it was restored. Even as eminent a figure as Horace Hutchinson was heavily outvoted when he proposed abandoning it in 1888. It lived on for another sixty-three years.

The stymie's departure in general has been approved but there have been voices, not least that of Bobby Jones, demanding that it should be restored. Some years after it was banished he wrote that he did not think it necessary that in matches each player must be able to play his own game free of any influence by his opponent, when the contest is head-to-head.

Jones mentioned two famous instances of the stymie, one which just conceivably cost Cyril Tolley his match against Jones in 1930 at St. Andrews. The other almost certainly accounted for Jack McLean in the final of the United States Amateur Championship against John Fischer in 1936, but on both occasions the sufferer could only blame himself. Jones claimed that the stymie emphasised the value of being closer to the hole with the approach and with the first putt. In his observation, and none has been wiser, the stymie more often than not was the means of enforcing a decision in favour of the more deserving player.

There was something to be said for allowing the stymie when a player stymied himself but this argument was overcome and in an age when there is a general trend towards eliminating luck, as far as possible, the stymie will never return. And never will there be the great satisfaction of negotiating one which a delicate skill often made possible. However its name is perpetuated in the form of a drink in the Royal and Ancient clubhouse. One day a member of the staff overheard someone say that stymies had been abolished. 'No Sir,' she said, 'we have some in the bar.'

A century after the first St. Andrews code the number of rules had increased only from 13 to 22; the tiny booklet was more like a 'carnet de bal.' The extra rules included the right to identify a ball when covered with bent, whins or sand, and to clear the putting green of loose impediments. Also the ball could be teed four to six club lengths from the hole instead of one. Another rule dealt at length with rubs of the green, such as a ball striking an opponent, his caddie or clubs, and vice versa. The general penalty of loss of hole for infringements not covered by the Rules was introduced in 1933.

One remarkable rule, which modern golfers might find amusing to try in a friendly match, was abandoned in 1857, and not surprisingly. It stated that if a player considered his ball unplayable he could, with the opponent's consent, lift, drop and lose a stroke. But if the opponent disagreed he himself then had to attempt to play the ball. If he made it playable within two strokes these counted against the original striker; if he failed after two blows then the original procedure was adopted. The rule did not forbid the recoverer from playing back toward the tee. The possible injustices of the rule, designed to prevent frivolous claims, were so obvious that it was soon abandoned.

Although the Royal and Ancient, by the end of the nineteenth century, had long been a principal influence in matters of the rules its authority was not established until 1897. Previously there had been concern that the game, which had expanded swiftly in England and elsewhere, lacked a controlling body. In May 1885 the secretary of Royal Wimbledon had suggested that the Royal and Ancient form an association of clubs, bound to accept one uniform code of rules, but the point went unheeded until 1896.

At a General Meeting of the Club that year Mr. Hall Blyth suggested a motion to be considered at Sandwich by the delegate clubs responsible for the Amateur championship. It was that all clubs should send a representative to a meeting in Edinburgh to discuss the formation of a Golf Union. The Royal and Ancient wanted no part of this but the delegates did discuss it during the championship at Sandwich. The outcome was that no support was given to proposals to create any rival authority to the R. & A. Furthermore the Club was asked to evolve a scheme for the election of a committee to deal with all questions of the Rules. It was therefore suggested that half the members of such a committee should be members of the Club and half should represent seven other clubs. These did not include the Edinburgh Burgess and the Royal Albert, Montrose which were much senior to most of the others. The two clubs strongly disapproved of the proposal and said that if they could not be represented then complete authority should rest with the Royal and Ancient.

The proposal was put before the General Meeting in September 1896 but an amendment by R. T. Boothby and F. G. Tait that it be not adopted was carried by 64 votes to 61. It seemed as if deadlock had been reached but at the next September Meeting the lively Hall Blyth moved that a new but not very different constitution be adopted. The members agreed and the Rules of Golf Committee was born.

Birth of the American Connection

When the United States Golf Association was formed in 1894 the Royal and Ancient were fortunate that one of its founders was Charles Blair Macdonald, a towering personality who had a great influence on the early growth of American golf. His passion for the game, and admiration for the British way of it, were born when his father, a prosperous citizen

of Chicago, sent his son, aged sixteen, to the University of St. Andrews.
The boy's grandfather was a member of the Club and the day after his
arrival young Charles, whose interest in golf until then had been slender,
was taken to Old Tom Morris's shop and fully equipped, as well as
being provided with a locker therein. No boy at that time could have
asked for a finer baptism.

Macdonald soon developed into a good golfer, accomplished enough
to play with Young Tom. In 1895 he won the first U.S. Amateur championship to be run by the U.S.G.A. Two years earlier he had designed
the first American 18 hole course, for the Chicago Club at Wheaton,
revealing an architectural skill unapproached by anyone in the United
States. In later years this skill was used to memorable effect in the
National Links on Long Island and Mid-Ocean in Bermuda. The
National was his masterpiece, intended to show his admiration of the
old British links. His loyalty to the Royal and Ancient never waned and
his insistence that its rules be precisely observed was not always met with
sympathy, but he was intelligent, articulate and rich, and so forceful was
his personality that he usually had his way. In 1897 he was one of those
appointed by the United States Golf Association to examine the rules. It
was decided that no change be made to the Royal and Ancient code, but
certain rules were added for the United States.

Had the Royal and Ancient sought an ambassador from among its
own members they could not have found one more influential than
Macdonald. In 1907 the Americans sought a revision of the St. Andrews
code and had the Rules of Golf Committee not agreed there might have
been a parting of the ways. To confirm their wish to avoid any division
they invited Macdonald, a member of the Club, to serve on the Committee. He accepted. The following year at a General Meeting the Committee recognised that where golf is played under conditions materially
different from those at St. Andrews and similar courses, the special
circumstances must be met by local bye-laws.

One interesting controversy of the Edwardian period concerned the
shape of the putter. This originated in 1904 when, to the great dismay of
British golfers, Walter Travis became the first foreign player to win in
Britain when he was Amateur champion at Sandwich. Although born
in Australia Travis was an American and had won the U.S. Amateur
title three times. He had played in Britain before but without much
success and was determined to win the championship. He was, it seems,
a cold, reserved person and not one to be deterred from his purpose by
social activities, then very much a part of the amateur scene. From what-

ever cause little affection existed between himself and the golfers at
Sandwich. When Travis arrived there after some three weeks at St.
Andrews and elsewhere his normal steady game had deserted him.
Eventually he recovered his rhythm but his putting, usually a great
strength, was still uncertain. On the eve of the championship he borrowed a Schenectady putter, its shaft centered in a mallet-shaped head,
from one of the American friends travelling with him, and thereafter
wrought havoc with it. His steadiness, relentless will and lethal putting
took him through several close matches and then, with something to
spare, he disposed of Harold Hilton, Horace Hutchinson and, in the
final, Edward Blackwell. It has been said that his moment of victory,
which must have been intensely satisfying to him, was at first greeted
with resounding silence.

The shock to British pride can be imagined and many must have
seen the Schenectady as an instrument of the devil but six years passed
before it was banned. Reaction was not, as has been supposed, one of
sudden pique because a foreigner had triumphed on hallowed ground.
In 1909 the Rules Committee received a query from New Zealand as
to whether a small croquet mallet was permissible for putting. The swift
answer was 'No' because the Committee were resolutely against any
substantial departure from the traditional form of the golf club.

The main point at issue regarding the putter was that the shaft must
be 'fixed to the heel, or to the neck socket or hosel which terminates at
the heel'. Thus in September 1910 the Schenectady or centre-shafted
putter was doomed until a meeting in 1951 when the Royal and Ancient
yielded to the U.S.G.A. regarding the putter, the head of which could
be fixed at any point in the head, and need not remain in line with the
heel. The same meeting also conceded the banning of the stymie after
several American requests. Naturally, the banning of the Schenectady
had not been approved in the United States where it was in common use
but a tactful letter from Charles Macdonald to the Rules Committee
helped avert a division between the two governing bodies. He quoted
one of the U.S.G.A. bye-laws which allowed certain local rules for competition in the United States and these could permit the use of centre-
shafted or mallet putters. The Rules Committee remained adamant on
their own ruling but there was no split with the U.S.G.A.

Unquestionably, the deepest and most enduring concern of both
governing bodies has been the power of the golf ball, and how best to
limit it. There was considerable argument when the gutty began to
supersede the feathery but the basis of this was commercial rather than

the length that could be achieved. The rubber-cored ball, invented by Coburn Haskell, an American golfer from Cleveland, proved a very different matter. In 1900 J. H. Taylor, who was touring the United States with Vardon, tried it for a few shots and regretted that he had not used it for the Open championship at Wheaton, in which Vardon beat him by two strokes. Slowly the use of the ball filtered over to Britain but not until 1902 did the whole golfing world become aware of its significance. In a practice round for the Open at Hoylake that summer Sandy Herd borrowed a Haskell from John Ball on the 15th: 'The first drive with the Haskell was longer than any I had ever made with the gutta. That was the end of the gutta for me'.

Herd won that Open and the gutty thereafter was doomed to a lingering death. The Haskell became the most desirable golfing object on earth and as Bernard Darwin wrote, 'the man with Haskells to sell had the world at his feet. Some virtue had gone from the game for ever, but it was a pleasanter and easier game'. The mass of golfers joyously welcomed the Haskell but a few experts regretted the passing of the gutty. Ten years after Herd's victory the great Vardon wrote that no period of the game had been so 'pregnant with evolution'. His words are still true, but he was convinced that the rubber-cored ball had done much to spoil golf as an athletic and scientific recreation.

This was a natural reaction because Vardon and the other great players were masters of the gutty, and could judge within a yard or so where it would pitch and stop. Accustoming themselves to allow for bounce and run was a problem but, as Vardon generously admitted, the rubber-core had increased the enjoyment of countless thousands as well as greatly helping to attract beginners to the game.

It seems that before the First World War the Royal and Ancient felt powerless to try and standardise the ball or limit its length. The manufacturers had leaped at the rising market and innumerable types of the new ball appeared. The earlier ones were large, floating and bramble-marked, but not of a common size or weight. Charles Macdonald gave his view that the capacity to float should be the criterion in standardising the ball. In this he was supported by Harold Hilton who, a few years later in 1911, was to be the first and quite possibly the last British amateur to win the United States championship. In a letter to Macdonald which dwelt on the question of the far-flying ball destroying the design of courses, he wrote, 'Why do they not make it a floating ball with no restrictions as to size? We would all be happy in three months'. His theory was that if the ball were too small and heavy it would not float, and if large and lighter its length would be restricted, but the competition for length was a raging tide by then. In 1912, the first of the heavy, tightly-wound balls, the Dunlop 31, appeared. It was followed by others but the battle for restraint was not joined until after the War.

An Historic Day in May

At a Business Meeting of the Club in 1919 John L. Low, Chairman of the Rules Committee, said that to preserve the balance between the power of the ball and the length of holes, and in order to retain the special features of the game, the power should be limited. Low, who had been a member of the Committee since its inception, was one of the most distinguished golfers and able legislators of his generation, alive to any threat to the true spirit and fine traditions of the game.

Soon after the appearance of the Haskell he had accused the legislators of being neither brave nor prompt enough to offer any proposal which could restore the balance of the game. He said that had they banned the use of balls containing india-rubber the 'inventive genius of our transatlantic friends would have been stopped'. One wonders for how long this might have been, but Low must have been greatly consoled when in September 1920 the suggestion of his Committee the previous year was adopted. It was resolved that from May 1, 1921, the weight of the ball should not exceed 1.62 ounces and that it should be not less than 1.62 inches in diameter. These specifications remained fundamental for all countries under allegiance to the Royal and Ancient Rules. The United States Golf Association were in full agreement with this, arguing that the players and not the inventors should guide the development of the game.

Even this did not satisfy certain notable players who suggested that experiments be carried out in the summer of 1922 with balls as large as 1.705 inches and of unrestricted weight. The Ball Sub-Committee of the Royal and Ancient said they were willing to organise special competitions for the various sizes of balls but this willingness was not to be taken as an intention to change from the specification already in force. The Committee were not convinced that a change was feasible and controversy over the ball continued until the great search for a uniform size, for universal use, began some forty years later.

The origin of this was the decision of the United States Golf Association in May 1929 to adopt an easier and pleasanter ball for the average golfer. For two years until the end of 1932 the American ball weighed 1.55 ounces and measured 1.68 inches, but thereafter the weight was increased to 1.62, the same as the British ball. During the thirties the difference between the balls was of no great concern to the mass of golfers. The development of air travel was in its infancy and only a minute number of golfers crossed the Atlantic either way.

Nonetheless in 1936 Robert Harris, Chairman of the Ball Sub-Committee, suggested that the size of the ball be increased to 1.68 inches. Nothing came of this nor, sadly, of a document prepared by his Committee for the Business Meeting in May 1946. Eight years earlier the Committee had canvassed the opinions of the home Golfing Unions and authorities overseas. They were practically unanimous in wanting a less powerful ball and in saying that a decision was urgently required from the Royal and Ancient. The Rules of Golf Committee, which embraced the vast experience of Harris himself, Bernard Darwin and Roger Wethered, among others, proposed that the American size ball be adopted.

The arguments which prevailed against the motion were to seem unduly cautious in the years that followed. There was concern that the American manufacturers might dominate the British market, also that the views of the Unions might have changed since the War, and that it would be against the wishes of the majority of golfers. Three members of the Rules Committee, who were local residents, recommended that the ball remain unchanged for a minimum of five years but it was decided to wait three years while further investigations were made. However a great opportunity had been lost. If the Royal and Ancient had not procrastinated, and had taken a positive decision in favour of the larger ball at a time when the game and the manufacturers were still finding their feet after the War a great deal of time, effort and expense would have been avoided. The research and experiments involved in the quest for a uniform ball, which were to last for years, would never have been necessary.

The two most significant events in golf since the beginning of the twentieth century were the arrival of the rubber-cored ball and of the steel shaft. They could be described as epoch-making because almost straightaway they ended one era for ever and began another.

The use of steel shafts was first legalised by the United States Golf Association in 1926 but was only allowed by the Royal and Ancient when for climatic or other reasons it was difficult to obtain good hickory. The Committee wanted to be certain that any new development would not be detrimental to the game's best interests. Eventually they realised that the use of steel would not be harmful and at the September

Meeting in 1929 the manufacture of steel shafts became legal.

Naturally the professionals were concerned, claiming that hardship and loss would be caused. They correctly foresaw that the age of the clubmaker as a craftsman, with rare exceptions, was over and that factory mass production would take his place. At first these fears may have been justified because steel shafts could endure for years while hickory were frequently vulnerable to breakage. Ultimately the financial balance for the professional was restored but, except for the tournament golfer and the eccentric, the skill and pride involved in creating a club specially for an individual were no longer needed.

It was said that the first Lord Birkenhead was persuaded by Archie Compston to change his old mixed set of wooden clubs for one of matched steel. Later he told Compston that he never went out without regretting having left the old set in his locker, because they were clubs of 'rare vintage'. Nowadays the phrase rarely applies except to putters, the the last evidence of the hickory age still in use. Snead did use the same driver for a great many years, Locke the same old hickory putter and Neil Coles put lasting trust in an ancient pitching club; these were notable exceptions.

One direct outcome of the increased liveliness of the rubber-cored ball was the problem of making it stop on greens which, before watering became commonplace, often had rock-hard surfaces. It was found that exaggerating the markings on the faces of iron clubs could produce greater backspin and stop. This had been noticed during the Open at St. Andrews in 1921 and again at Troon where a deal of anxious filing took place on the eve of the championship. Clubs with over pronounced markings had been declared illegal in 1921. Ten years later clubs with faces more markedly concave than those hitherto in use were banned.

Before the Ryder Cup match at Ganton in 1949 Bernard Darwin, Chairman of the Rules Committee, was interrupted at dinner by a request from Ben Hogan, the American captain, that he examine the British players' clubs. He did so, remarking that there was nothing a little filing would not put right.

During the twenties a fearsome tendency was developing. There was then no limit on the number of clubs a golfer could use in a round. For generations the British had found that a dozen or less were sufficient, but technological minds in America were beginning a trend towards buying shots in a professional's shop by having an absurd number of clubs. When Lawson Little won the Amateur championship at Prestwick for the first time he was said to have a set of twenty or more, five of which were pitching clubs. The threat of an unlimited number of clubs becoming fashionable must have horrified every thinking golfer, but, as with the arrival of steel, there was anxiety among the professionals.

Early in 1937 Commander Charles Roe, long the devoted Secretary of the Professional Golfer's Association, wrote to the Royal and Ancient saying the proposal to reduce the number to 14 was undesirable and unnecessary. Fortunately the Club did not agree and in September 1938 the maximum of 14 clubs was declared the legal limit. Golfers are prone to imitation and can be extremely gullible concerning their own golf. Whereas some first class golfers might benefit from having innumerable clubs, it would only cause confusion among average players not to mention an awesome burden for anyone foolish enough to carry them. The decision to limit clubs was one of the most important ever taken by the Club. The Americans, who had started the disastrous fashion, apparently were the first to realise its dangers and the tendency towards mechanising the game. The United States Golf Association limited the number of clubs to 14 from January 1, 1938 but, strangely, a similar proposal by the Rules of Golf Committee was outvoted by Royal and Ancient members at the 1937 Business Meeting. This was a very rare instance of the Committee failing to gain approval, but a sufficient number of Members came to their senses in time for the limit to come into force on May Day 1939.

Once golf had recovered from the worst legacies of the Second World War and was on the threshold of a booming era it was clear that the manufacturers of clubs and balls, and the scientists who served them with increasing ingenuity, could have a mounting influence. Competition between the companies intensified and power was the soul of the plot. Unless restrained within reasonable bounds the effect on the game could have been harmful.

Constant vigilance by the governing bodies was, and remains, essential particularly with the swift development of synthetics. This was reflected in the sixties with the appearance of shafts made of fibre-glass and carbon graphite. Aluminium also was tried. The quest for lightness of shafts without loss of strength, and extra length from the ball, within the limits of the Rules, became continuing subjects for research. This involved considerable expense but markets were expanding, and at their heart was the golfer ever striving, longing for more length.

The main concern was the ball and in February 1968 an *ad hoc* joint Royal and Ancient and United States Golf Association Ball Committee was formed. Its main purpose was to see whether a ball of uniform size was feasible for use throughout the world. The project was expected to last several years because it was appreciated that no acceptable decision to amend the specification of the ball could be taken without the collaboration of manufacturers and golfers throughout the world. Donald Smith, later a Captain of the Club, was chairman for the Royal and Ancient and Edward Emerson for the United States Golf Association. Seven years earlier the Royal and Ancient had canvassed opinion from its sphere of influence as to whether the larger ball, (hereafter named the 1.68), should replace the smaller (1.62). The response, partly through indifference and resistance to change, was not in favour. The handicap golfer in Britain, the United States and elsewhere was content with the ball as it was. The Club, not being an autocracy, was unwilling to enforce a change when there was no great demand. Also, British manufacturers, who had the 1.62 market almost entirely to themselves, would face much greater competition at home and abroad from American firms. It was argued too that the 1.68 ball would be vulnerable to the heavy winds that frequently swept the seaside courses, making the game more difficult especially for the elderly and for women golfers. Overmuch was made of this because Britain is the only country in the world where a considerable amount of golf is played in these conditions. At the same time many accomplished golfers and observers who had watched golf in the United States believed that the advantages of the 1.68 outweighed those of the 1.62. The 1.68 demanded more accurate striking for maximum effect, offered greater flexibility of control and, save in adverse winds, the difference in length was not too great. Most people agreed that it was an easier ball for the game around the greens and for putting. The Royal and Ancient however were not to be persuaded into impulsive action by a minority and insisted on a democratic approach to the problem. Meanwhile the Professional Golfers Association, largely through concern over American supremacy, decided to experiment with the 1.68 and it was made compulsory for all their main events in 1964. A questionnaire to 276 tournament players revealed a majority in favour of the 1.68 but the trial was abandoned until 1968 when it was decided to use the 1.68 for all official tournaments for the following three years. Thereafter the players were convinced that it was the better ball for them and there was no question of a return to the 1.62. The Professional Golfers Association had given a brave lead, and doubtless the Royal and Ancient were grateful for the evidence.

In the autumn of 1970 the Joint Ball Committee announced their agreement that a uniform ball was feasible. After various tests by

machines and in play involving close co-operation with the manufacturers, it was found that a 1.65 ball, halfway between the two sizes, resembled the 1.62 too closely. Experiments with 1.66 revealed that it
was more suitable for the purpose and it was hoped that after further
tests it could be introduced, possibly by 1973. Within three years this
project was dying. The attitude of the manufacturers of the larger ball
had made it impossible for the United States Golf Association to proceed
with the 1.66 ball. Although most anxious to make this ball legal, they
would have become vulnerable to the anti-trust laws involving restric-
tion of trade.

The American manufacturers had proposed that a scientific and
technical programme be carried out at considerable cost over a long
period in order to discover what they thought was the most suitable
uniform size of ball. After lengthy examination the United States Golf
Association rejected the proposal and advised the Royal and Ancient that
the uniform ball programme had to be abandoned. In the end the whole
debate was concerned with one-fiftieth of an inch. The difference between the 1.66 and 1.68 balls is scarcely visible. Had even the latter
become the uniform ball, gradually superseding the 1.62, there is little
doubt golfers would soon have forgotten all about the difference.

The Royal and Ancient was thus left in an invidious position. All its
affiliated unions throughout the world and the British Professional
Golfers Association had agreed in 1972 that they would accept the 1.66
ball but because of the Americans' problem it was no longer feasible.
While awaiting the decision several professional bodies in other countries
had followed the example of the British and had turned to the 1.68 ball.
The Championship Committee therefore decided in December 1973 that
this ball should be compulsory for the Open at Lytham the following
summer, and so it has remained.

The decision was taken without reference to a Business Meeting
which would have involved waiting six months until the following
May. This caused considerable discussion, even anger, among Members
who claimed that the rules of the Club had been infringed. Some also
did not think that the use of the 1.62 ball should have been banned.
There were many complaints to the Chairman of the General Committee and criticism of W. M. Miller and his Championship Committee.
There was even talk of a censure motion but this was avoided when an
explanation was given at the ensuing May Meeting. The main point was
whether the decision was covered by the right of the Championship
Committee to stipulate conditions for the Open. After all they were not

contracting outside the Rules of Golf; the 1.68 ball was legal. The decision was justified not least because the majority of competitors in the Open played the 1.68 ball throughout the year.

As the Joint Ball Committee had then become redundant an Implements and Ball Committee was created to deal with all matters arising under Rule 2 concerning the Club and the Ball and, most important, to hold a close watching brief on developments in club and ball manufacture, particularly as to the length the ball could be hit. To this end the Royal and Ancient decided to introduce in January 1976 a velocity test similar to that used by the United States Golf Association. It had long been overdue in Britain. No sooner had the Royal and Ancient taken this step than the United States Golf Association introduced an Overall Distance Standard which only they could operate. Since the first basic rule regarding the making of clubs declared that the head must not contain 'any mechanical contrivance such as springs' the Rules Committee have always rejected any form of trick equipment, alien to the spirit of the game. Over the years countless types of clubs and balls have been banned to the chagrin of their designers, including the inventor of the 'bleeper' ball. Millions of golfers when searching for their ball have cursed it for not giving a sign as to its whereabouts. An electronic core, similar in practice to a metal detector, made this possible. When the player, equipped with an instrument, approached the ball it was supposed to give signals.

The ball contravened the Rule of no outside aid for the golfer and was deemed an artificial device. Obviously it could give the owner an unfair advantage, and could have set a precedent. Remote control by radio is commonplace and in an age of extraordinary electronic miracles it might not be beyond the inventiveness of someone to apply the principle to a golf ball. Doubtless at first the device would be expensive, but when a long slice was soaring out of bounds what a joy it would be to guide it smoothly back to the fairway or, for that matter, hole the long putt which clearly was going to miss. This might be far-fetched but the appearance in 1976 of the Polara ball, invented by two Californian scientists, posed a more delicate problem. They claimed that their ball, with an unusual aerodynamic design, was 'designed to fly straighter and longer from tee to green' but the United States Golf Association banned it because the dimple pattern caused the ball to perform in a manner which reduced golf skill and was not in the best interests of the game. An action for damages resulted against the United States Golf Association and the United States manufacturers.

Considering the climatic, economic and social differences between Britain and America, as they affect golf, the two governing bodies have contrived to keep in step remarkably well, particularly since their meeting in London in 1951. This conference was of great significance to the universal welfare of the game. It was the first of the quadrennial meetings between the Americans and British, and delegates from Australia and Canada were also present. One of their principal terms of reference was that 'the perspective was to be world-wide, to meet the varying conditions under which the game is now played'. A unified Code of Rules was agreed upon. The stymie was abolished and the penalty for out of bounds, lost or unplayable balls was finally established as stroke and distance. This had been the ruling for a lost ball in the very first Code; the other contingencies were not considered in the Rules until a century or more later, and from time to time there were changes. For thirty years from 1920 the penalties had been stroke and distance for all three occurrences then, in 1950, as an experiment after a postal vote had been taken, the penalties were reduced to distance only. In 1934 the Royal and Ancient had resisted a request from the United States Golf Association that this ruling be adopted.

Bernard Darwin was Chairman of the Rules Committee in 1949 and asked that the reduced penalties be given a two year trial. Some may have wondered whether his personal passion concerning the traditional way of playing the game did not conflict with the decision he announced on behalf of his Committee. In his preface to the proposed Code he wrote that the opinion of governing bodies at home and abroad, and of Club members, was in favour. This prompted forthright criticism from Robert Harris who had served on the Rules Committee for twenty years until 1946. He saw no reason for change, considered that it created a new and different game and that it would 'effectively undermine the very fundamentals of the game besides entirely destroying that feeling which inspires all real golfers to exert their best efforts in the face of difficulties'. The flaws in the experiment were soon revealed, notably in the Open at Troon when Roberto De Vicenzo bunkered his tee shot to the short 8th. He declared the ball unplayable, hit a good second shot to the green and holed his putt for a three, having avoided all the dangers inherent in the bunkers on either side of the narrow green. Distance only for 'out of bounds' gave a clear advantage to the powerful player who could afford to let fly, knowing that if he failed he would only be playing two from the tee. Two years later the experiment ended.

Rarely since has a rule been abandoned or introduced within the quadrennial period. An exception was the one which decreed that in stroke play the ball could be cleaned only once on the green and that putting should be continuous. This was introduced in 1968 in the hope that it would quicken play and reduce the number of times a ball was lifted on the green. The rule was neither popular, easy to enforce, nor, in some instances, was it always fair. On one day of a tournament a player might have perfectly dry conditions, while another might face heavy dew or rain and possibly mud. When two players were in close combat in a stroke play competition one of them might gain a considerable advantage by holing out first when he was closest to the hole, thus defying a basic principle of the game. An example of this occurred in 1968 on the last green at the very end of the World Team championship in Melbourne. Britain were one stroke behind the United States. After three good shots Ronnie Shade was six feet from the hole; Siderowf, who had not played the hole as well as his opponent was a yard from it in four having putted once. Under the rule he had to putt again and holed for a five. Shade missed and the United States won the Eisenhower Trophy. Had the proper rule obtained then, Shade, as he deserved, would have attempted to hole out first and, whether he succeeded or not, the pressure upon Siderowf would have been intensified. This Rule was abandoned at the end of 1969.

A paramount concern of the law makers has always been to preserve the traditional method of playing the game. In 1968, when putting croquet fashion with the stance astride the line was banned, the Committee met some fierce criticism from those who, using this method, had found salvation from the dreaded 'twitch', or others who simply found it more effective. The Royal and Ancient were condemned for sabotaging the enjoyment of the elderly and the anxious, but they stood firm. Those who complained had a splendid example in Snead to encourage them. He changed to the sideways croquet method with little if any loss of effect.

In 1975 the Rules forbade a caddie to stand or crouch behind the player while he was putting. This practice had been pursued in Britain notably by Hubert Green and Johnny Miller. It was not thought that these two distinguished American golfers were trying to gain an unfair advantage but clearly there could be occasions when the caddie's close presence, like a baseball catcher, with or without umbrella, could provide helpful shelter. In any event it did not look right.

The Rules of Golf have been criticised, not least through the wit of the late Henry Longhurst, for being too lengthy and too involved to remember or even, on occasion, to understand. In the beginning they were not designed to eliminate chance. The player measured himself against the hazards of lie and nature, and fortune was balanced in the end. As John Low remarked in 1912, 'Some men are in a mutual spirit with the game and, though they know nothing about the Rules of Golf, they never have any difficulty in knowing the proper thing to do when some perplexing situation arises'. Sadly this does not apply to every golfer. As competition spread, with the onrush of commercial influences in its train, the law makers saw it as their duty to specify as clearly as possible what a golfer could, and could not do. No amount of forensic skill can cover every eventuality and there have been many occasions when strict adherence to the laws has been totally opposed to the spirit of the game. One instance involved Kel Nagle in the 1969 Alcan tournament. He failed to notice that the marker had put his total for the inward half in the space reserved for the 18th hole score. The aberration cost Nagle 31 strokes. For a while the absurd penalty for having more than 14 clubs in stroke play was two strokes for every hole they were carried. This once cost a well-known amateur 36 strokes and his team a qualifying place in a tournament.

Once the law and not the spirit rules there can be no exceptions. Nevertheless it is a rare tribute to an ancient game, and to those who have guided its destiny, that for all the expansion of the Rules there have not been many fundamental changes. It has retained its unique character and meaning, and the spirit in which all but a tiny minority play it.

Amateur Status

Many years before the first Amateur championship was played at Hoylake in 1885 John Ball, who was to become the supreme amateur golfer of the age, finished sixth in the Open championship and received a prize of ten shillings. He was still a boy and asked his mentor, Jack Morris, the Hoylake professional, what he should do with it. Morris told him to keep it, as anyone would have done. The amateur golfer had not then been defined in the Rules. Nor had he in 1885 when Douglas Rolland, a stone mason from Elie and not a regular professional, entered for the Amateur, though he had taken second prize in the Open the previous year. Clearly Rolland was not an amateur but the Committee recalled the case of Ball, who was approaching the heights as a player. That year Ball reached the semi-final of the Amateur championship which he was to win eight times. The Committee, faced with what might have been an embarrassing situation, made a wise decision which was to guide the

Royal and Ancient when Amateur status was in question. It was based on Ball's youth when he received his prize, and also that he had not done anything to transgress the accepted definition of an amateur.

The distinction between amateur and professional was clearly marked until after the First World War when economic and social distinctions began a process of erosion which accelerated swiftly after the Second World War. Throughout the years when golf was gradually expanding from its beginning as a private Scottish pastime, the amateur played for relaxation as he is supposed to do now. The only money involved was in token prizes and wagers. Those who could not afford to play did not play. There was no call for sponsors, expenses or the finding of loopholes in the Rules for gimmicky events with ridiculous prizes.

Professional tournaments, apart from the Open, did not exist until the twentieth century. The professional golfer relied on challenge and exhibition matches to capitalise his skill and was readily identifiable. There was none of the wandering between two worlds which has afflicted so many golfers in the past twenty years or so with the onrush of commercialism. The Royal and Ancient therefore were rarely called upon for a decision as to the status of a golfer, and the United States Golf Association probably took the lead in making a legal distinction between the amateur and the professional.

After Francis Ouimet had become an instant American hero with his famous victory in 1913 he was besieged with offers which, as Herbert Warren Wind tells, would have netted him $15,000. Ouimet, however, had promised that he would join a friend in opening a sporting goods store. Although Ouimet was warned that he would lose his amateur status if he did so he was determined to keep his word. The United States Golf Association rule was strict, defining the professional as a person engaged in any business concerned with golf. Ouimet therefore was declared a professional from January 1916 and the United States Golf Association was most unpopular. As Wind remarked, had Ouimet chosen to evade the rule he could easily have accepted jobs from wealthy admirers, but he was an honourable man, a person of sterling character and a true amateur. He was re-instated after two years.

None of this concerned the Royal and Ancient; most golfers at the time were involved with more urgent affairs in France and no amateur golfer of stature comparable with Ouimet had given the Club cause to exercise their minds as to his amateur status. Few indeed turned professional after achieving prominence as an amateur. The outstanding exception was Philip Perkins, who won the English and British

championships before going to the United States where he was successful both as an amateur and as a professional. Only Jones stood between
him and winning the Amateur championship, and a year or so later after
turning professional he finished second to Sarazen in the 1932 Open.

Eminent amateurs remained on their side of the fence until the two
finest Scottish players of the period, Jack McLean in 1936 and Hector
Thomson in 1940, turned professional. In the thirties Joyce Wethered
(later Lady Heathcoat-Amory) and Enid Wilson lost their amateur status
for a while but that was after their distinguished championship careers
were over. The temptation for a good amateur to become a professional
was also tempered by the severely restrictive Professional Golfers Association rule that such a player had to wait five years before receiving prize
money in official Professional Golfers Association events. So the Royal
and Ancient was not beset with the vexed question as to what an amateur may do without losing his status as such.

Apparently, the possibility of problems ahead was foreseen by the
Rules Committee in May 1947. A paragraph concerning Amateur Status
was added to the Rules, but such matters were dealt with by a Sub-
Committee of the Championship Committee. Almost twenty years
passed before an Amateur Status Committee, with Gerald Micklem as
Chairman, was formed. Two years later his Committee of five members
was given full and separate status. It has operated closely with the United
States Golf Association and with affiliated Unions and Associations.
Although the Royal and Ancient and the United States Golf Association
Rules are as uniform as possible, there are exceptions in both Codes due
to different social and geographical conditions.

The considerations facing Micklem's Committee and those of his
successors, became increasingly complex. It was thought in some quarters that the problem of Amateur Status would be more readily resolved
by defining the professional and regarding everyone else as amateurs. In
the early seventies a detailed study of this idea was made. It was abandoned mainly because it was considered that there would be as many
'borderline' cases as under the Rule then in force, and that it would pre-
judice the aim of uniformity with the United States Golf Association.

As standards of teaching improved and the Golf Foundation rapidly
expanded, an ever-increasing number of good young golfers emerged.
At the same time the cost of competing in the main amateur events was
soaring beyond the means of many, if not most, young men. Naturally
their thoughts turned towards a professional career, particularly as prize
money was mounting year by year. Jacklin, and to a lesser extent others,

had shown that riches awaited those with the essential character and ability which, of course, the majority did not have.

The number of applications for re-instatement as amateurs increased to as many as 125 in 1978. The majority are granted but the waiting period can range from two to ten years according to the player's experience as a professional. In 1978 the position was modified so that a player, having failed in his first attempt to gain a Tournament Player's Card and having done nothing else as a professional, might only have to wait six months, but under the Rules only one re-instatement is possible. The Committee were adopting a more liberal attitude towards amateur status, essential if golf, unlike other games, was not to abandon the distinction between amateur and professional. Furthermore in 1974 J. E. Behrend, Chairman of the Committee, announced that a prize voucher could be used for any retail purpose and not necessarily for the purchase of golf equipment. This assisted many young players who were finding it difficult to remain in the amateur game. The United States Golf Association did not follow this lead which could be said to be the Royal and Ancient answer to the American College Scholarships which give a player abundant golf for several years with expenses paid. The Royal and Ancient may approve the occasional scholarship but they enforce stricter academic qualifications. The Committee came to recognise the great value to the amateur game of sponsorship provided its funds were channelled through official Unions who can enforce the Rules by controlling the way in which the money is used.

After March 1978 the Rule forbidding an amateur to sell golf merchandise because of his skill or reputation, was abolished by the Royal and Ancient and the United States Golf Association. Both bodies realised that such a practice was not inherently contrary to the concept of an amateur golfer, many of whom linked their business with the game.

The Committee appreciated also that rules were of no avail unless they could be enforced. The one which, before March 1978, forbade an amateur to accept golf equipment without paying the current market price was a good example. How could this possibly be prevented? As long as the player's name was not used for advertising it was considered that the receipt of free goods by an amateur would find its own level, but such goods were not to include gifts or prizes such as cars. The amateur who won a car and profited accordingly would lose his status, and would have to wait a long time if he wished to regain it.

In his report to the Members at the Business Meeting in September 1978, Michael Bonallack the Chairman, emphasised that his Committee were ever mindful of the definition of an amateur as 'One who plays the game as a non-remunerative or non-profit making sport'. This principle had not been transgressed by introducing a more lenient approach to the Rules. The Royal and Ancient was keeping pace with the times.

CHAPTER TEN

THE PROFESSIONALS

'They may shut up their shops and toll their bells, for the greatest among them is gone.' The words, spoken by a Member of the Club, echoed the feelings of St. Andrews golfers and others from afar when Allan Robertson died in 1859. He was the first of the great professionals, a calling which hitherto had not been clearly defined. On the other hand ball making had been a recognised craft since 1618. James I, as James VI of Scotland, had been well aware of golf, and was concerned at the money leaving the kingdom for the purchase of balls from Holland. He therefore granted a monopoly of ball making to James Melvill and William Berwick to last for twenty years. Others followed, notably John Gourlay, famous for the manufacture of the feathery. When Allan Robertson was born in 1815 his family had long been established in a business which the boy naturally joined. It was said that from childhood Allan's playthings were golf clubs. His style was easy and graceful and he used long, light clubs with such control that he could pretend to be hitting a powerful shot whereas he was sparing it, thus deceiving the opponent. He relied on accuracy and placing rather than length, he was a golfer who played the percentages. 'His deadly steadiness was conspicuous with thoughtful consideration.' He was the Hogan of his time, and withal blessed with a cheerful serenity and a sense of superiority to circumstance.

Robertson was a smallish man, sturdily built, with reddish side whiskers, who wore an almost perpetual smile and a red coat while playing. Tom Morris described him as 'the cunningest bit body of a player that ever handled club, cleek or putter. A kindly body with just a wealth of sly, pawky fun about him.' It is easy to realise what a hero he must have been to the golfers at St. Andrews.

A contemporary writer asked, 'Who that has once seen the champion golfer can ever forget him? Our scene is the St. Andrews links on a genial summer day. Allan's house crowns the summit of the slope, down towards the sea − the beautiful sea − lies the white Club-House, with its gravelled terrace. It is not yet eleven, that great hour of cause on the links. Suddenly a golfer appears at the Club-House door; he looks about for somebody who is evidently lacking. "Where's Allan?". The cry is repeated by telegraphic caddies right up to the champion's little garden (where the Golf Hotel dining room once was). A minute elapses and down comes the champion in hot haste to the Club-house.' For all his repute Allan was being summoned; members of those days did not attend upon their heroes. 'Now the match is arranged. Allan had evidently got to nurse an elementary golfer. Allan and his protegé against two rather good hands. Remark how pleasant the little man is; no miss of his partner causes a shade to his habitual good nature, and ten to one when the match comes in, the new player swears by Allan, and gives in his adhesion to golf once and for all'.

Robertson may have been something of a pioneer for his part in introducing iron clubs for approach shots which previously had been played with baffing spoons. He had a name for all his clubs, among them Sir David Baird, the Doctor, Sir Robert Peel and the Frying Pan, a broad-bladed iron for use in bunkers. One of his lasting claims to fame was a round of 79, the first under 80 on the Old Course, played a year before his death. At the time it must have seemed a miraculous score for the greens were 'in the rough' and the bunkers in their natural state.

It was claimed for Robertson that he, alone in the annals of the pastime, was never beaten. This was not strictly true for Tom Morris beat him twice, once by 3 and 2 in a small money match and again when the stake was a red coat. Robertson's excuse on this occasion was that all the way round he thought the wee coatie would fit Tom better. The coat was given by J. Wolfe Murray who was Captain in 1848, a notable archer and, when using a bow and arrow, beat Young Tom Morris who was playing with clubs and ball. This must have been one of the first, if not *the* first of such challenge matches. Wolfe Murray played golf almost to the end of his life, riding the links on a white pony, mounting and dismounting between shots and employing one caddie for the horse and another for his clubs. A splendid vision he must have made.

Tom once challenged Allan to a match for £100 but it was never accepted. Allan was not the last great golfer to realise that he had more to lose than to gain by risking his reputation in such a contest; certainly he was more than willing to have Morris as a partner. They were invincible in foursomes. The most famous of their matches was against the brothers Dunn, Willie and James, over three courses. On their home links at Musselburgh the Dunns slaughtered their mighty opponents by

13 and 12. Morris and Robertson won narrowly at St. Andrews but at North Berwick were four down and eight to play. They recovered and were all square when at the 17th a second shot pulled under a rock cost the Dunns the hole. The St. Andrews golfers won £400, not to mention any share of the twenty to one odds that had been laid against them when they were far behind. The money at stake was riches indeed for those days and there was no mention of a prize for the losers, as inevitably there would be in the modern, cushioned age.

For a while before his death Robertson was charged with superintending the improvement of the Old Course greens. In 1856 the Royal and Ancient had voted a sum of £25 for this purpose. Then early in 1859 Robertson contracted jaundice and after a gradual decline died on 1st September that year. The Club passed the following resolutions: 'This meeting has heard with deep regret of the death of Allan Robertson, and they desire to record on their minutes the opinion, universally entertained, of the almost unrivalled skill with which he played the game of golf, combining a ready and correct judgement with most accurate execution. They desire also to express the sense of the propriety of his whole conduct, and unvarying civility with which he mingled with all classes of golfers, of his cordiality to those of his own, of his integrity, his happy temper and the anxiety he always manifested to promote the comfort of all who frequented the Links.'

The Union Club also were anxious to acknowledge Robertson's eminent part in improving the game and extending its practice throughout the Kingdom. A subscription, to which the Royal and Ancient contributed £25, was organised for his widow. In tribute to Robertson the *Dundee Advertiser* remarked that, 'A new era is about to dawn on the golfing links; the old stars are paling; when will others arise? Hugh Philp who knew how to make a club is gone; gone too, fine Allan, who knew how to handle one.' Little can the writer have appreciated that a new era was already in being which was to last for half a century until the death of Tom Morris, and its impress on the history of the Club would endure throughout the ages.

Tom Morris was born in St. Andrews in June 1821, the son of a letter carrier. As soon as he could walk he was hitting stones with a stick, and from a tender age would be on the links with any kind of club and ball he could get. When 18 he was apprenticed to Allan Robertson as a maker of clubs and feathery balls and remained with him for eleven years. During this period they played their great matches together but the advent of the gutta-percha ball led to a difference between them. Robertson was afraid that the new ball would threaten his business. 'He would buy up all the old balls and burn the "dirt". He was scornful of its performance and on one occasion deliberately topped it, remarking that it would not fly, but Robertson was no fool. He soon discovered that the gutty could be manufactured in far greater numbers and with less effort than the feathery.

This was the first great turning point in the development of the ball. Because it was so much cheaper and more durable the gutty encouraged the spread of the game which otherwise would have remained an exclusive pastime for the prosperous. Half a century later the appearance of the rubber-core ball caused more lasting controversy. Tom Morris experienced both these historic changes and became an historic figure himself. After the dispute with Robertson, Morris started his own business as a club and ball manufacturer but three years later was persuaded by Colonel Fairlie, who inspired the founding of the Open championship, to be custodian of the links at Prestwick. There Morris remained for fourteen years in spite of many pleas for his return to St. Andrews. He preferred the 12 hole links to the Old Course. This was hardly surprising. After finishing second to Willie Park in the first Open he won the next two.

Morris might have stayed longer at Prestwick but for a proposal at the Autumn Meeting of the Royal and Ancient in 1863 that a professional golfer should be employed by the Club and be entirely responsible for the upkeep of the course. A large majority supported R. T. Boothby's proposal and at the General Meeting in May 1864 it was decided that 'Thomas Morris of Prestwick, formerly of St. Andrews, be brought here as professional golfer at a salary of (£50) fifty pounds a year, on the understanding that he shall have entire charge of the golf course, and be responsible for it being kept in proper order, and that he shall be the servant of the Club under the direction and control of the Committee in charge of the green.'

Morris duly reported at a full meeting of Members in the Clubhouse. He was given a detailed account of his duties and handed a barrow, a shovel and a spade. Little is known of Tom's skill as a greenkeeper except that sand, and more sand, was to be his principle remedy. In this he was wise and doubtless much of the rest was left to nature. He was not beset with science and those artificial processes which occasionally nowadays do more harm than good. For almost forty years Morris was a devoted servant of the Club and, apart from his skill as a player which brought him four victories in the early Opens, was loved and respected by everyone. In the words of A. J. S. Everard 'Nobility of character is writ on his handsome sunburnt face in letters clear as day, and withal there is an admixture of naive, unsophisticated simplicity which is charming to the last degree'.

Until the genius of his son, Young Tom, began to flower Tom was probably the finest golfer of his time. In an age when the majority of swings were uninhibited furious attacks on the ball, his swing was comparatively slow and enabled him to use more supple clubs than those of his rivals. If he had a weakness it was in short putting and this prompted his son to the unfilial remark that if the hole were a yard nearer his Father would be a good putter. Old Tom once received a letter addressed to the 'Misser of short Putts, Prestwick', and the postman had no doubt as to its destination. No such frailty beset his son. Young Tom was the first golfer to change an old order of things substantially. He scored in the seventies far more frequently than anyone had ever done. His total of 149 at Prestwick when he won his third successive Open, twelve strokes ahead of his closest pursuers must have astounded all golfers. The score was never approached while the championship was played over 36 holes, and it remained relatively unbeaten until thirty years later when the rubber-cored ball began to revolutionise the game. In those early years the twelve holes at Prestwick measured some 3800 yards and the competitor played three rounds in one day. Considering that Young Tom was using the gutty ball, and remembering the nature of his clubs and the condition of the links, which modern golfers would consider unplayable, his feat was nothing short of marvellous.

Contemporary accounts of Young Tom's golf are scarce and there are no pictures of him playing. He was uncommonly strong and although his swing did not have the smoothness of that of some of the other good players, David Strath for example, it was more compact and he hit the ball very hard. He was a long driver but his strength was most remarkable in the length he achieved with his niblick, a 'rather prosy and unpromising sort of instrument', from bad lies which must in those days have abounded. If Allan Robertson was the man who began the trend of using an iron instead of a baffing spoon, Young Tom was the man who emphasised it. His iron play was said to be magnificent and he was particularly good into a gale of wind. As if these virtues were not enough he was a great putter, always attacking the hole with a wooden club and the ball very close to his right toe. Seemingly he was as painstaking as Nicklaus in his approach to the shortest of putts. No wonder he was supreme and his death at the early age of only 24 is one of the saddest of all golfing tales.

One autumn day in 1875 Young Tom was playing with his father against the Park brothers at North Berwick, when a telegram arrived from St. Andrews reporting that Young Tom's wife had died after giving birth to their first child. Old Tom received the telegram and told his son only that they must return immediately. A yacht was loaned for the journey across the Forth but Old Tom spared his son the news until harbour was reached. A parson, who was in the Morris House when the men arrived, wrote 'I never forget the poor young man's stony look; stricken was not the word; and how, all of a sudden, he started up and cried, "It is not true", I have seen many sorrowful things but not like that Saturday night'. Young Tom never recovered from the tragedy. His natural gaiety vanished and well though he continued to play his heart was not in it, and his health declined. On Christmas Eve he supped with his friends, returned home and talked a while with his mother before retiring. The following morning he was found dead in bed. It was said that he died of a broken heart but the cause was found to be a burst artery in a lung. The grief that spread through the golfing world that Christmas needs no imagining. He was buried in the cathedral church-yard and the inscription on his memorial reads – 'He thrice won the Champion belt and held it without rivalry, and yet without envy, his many amiable qualities being no less acknowledged than his golfing achievements'.

More than thirty years were to pass before Old Tom joined his son in the churchyard. His indestructible spirit survived the loss of his greatest pride and greatest golfing partner, and later that of his remaining son James and of his only daughter. But his skill at the game endured. In 1901 when 80 he played the links in 86, probably the closest that any-one then had ever come to matching his age, a not uncommon feat in modern times. Five years earlier at Muirfield he had played in his last Open, perhaps the oldest man ever to compete in it. The previous summer, 1895, a Committee of the Club was appointed to consider a proposal to give Morris a testimonial. This actually occasioned an Extra-ordinary General Meeting at which the Club voted £100 towards the fund. A year later the fund amounted to £1240; Morris was thus assured of an income of over £100 a year in addition to his fees from other sources, including keeping the green, a post he did not resign until 1903. The Club then decided that his salary of £50 a year should remain for life. It was unchanged for almost 40 years, with no talk in those days of inflation, differentials, rates for the job and so on. Morris continued to be consulting Greenkeeper and to afford assistance on Medal Days and there may still be some living who can recall the splendid old figure taking the flag on the 18th green which bears his name.

Early in 1903 Morris gave a last sitting to Sir George Reid, RSA, in Edinburgh for a portrait commissioned by the Members of the Club. This portrait now hangs in the main room and it was said that on one of the artist's visits to St. Andrews Morris was invited to give his opinion of the portrait and remarked 'You've got the checks in my cap a' wrong'.

Old Tom died shortly before his 87th birthday leaving an imperishable name that stood for all the finest qualities to be sought in a professional golfer. His funeral was probably the largest ever seen in St. Andrews. The crowds were enormous; the shops were closed, blinds drawn in every house along the route to the Cathedral, and flags flew at half mast. Professors from the University and Members of the Club were in the procession. The Earl of Stair, the Captain, was one of the pallbearers and the greenkeeper carried the silver club and balls. The bronze medallion of Tom Morris was placed in its position on September 14, 1910 on the west gable of the Clubhouse and bears the following; 'Tom Morris, 1821–1908'. It had also been arranged to endow a bed in the Memorial Cottage Hospital, St. Andrews, for which professional golfers and caddies were offered preference. The Club had indeed been blessed in Morris, but were hardly less fortunate in his successors.

Andrew Kirkaldy, who served as Club professional from 1910 to 1933, was another distinctive personality although of a different order to Old Tom. He was a fine golfer (with a swing that hit the ball like the shutting of a knife) particularly at match play and as far back as 1878 he had been second in the Open. Kirkaldy was famous for his blunt, dour manner and his comments, many of which were unprintable. Bernard Darwin wrote of him that many of his supposed witticisms were, he imagined, uttered in deadly earnest. Kirkaldy may well have originated the remark that the door is shut when a player becomes dormy. In a famous challenge match against J. H. Taylor at St. Andrews Kirkaldy was one up on the last tee and said in a loud voice to Taylor, 'That's the door locked, Taylor, you canna beat me now'. In 1891 his brother Hugh, who died when he was 30, won the Open at St. Andrews with what was then the record score of 166 for 36 holes on the Old Course. Andrew won a play-off with Willie Fernie for second place and so for the first and only time brothers took the first two places in the Open. His manner probably stemmed from a harsh upbringing. His Father was a miner and a pensioner of the Crimean War and had to caddy in his old age to keep his family alive. This prompted Andrew to write in his

reminiscences 'There is one thing the Old Country can never be proud
of that is the way the soldier has been praised when he was wanted and
starved when not wanted'. Kirkaldy also recalled a fact, not generally
known, that the 18th green was built up from a rubbish heap that had
also served as a burial ground. When his father worked as a labourer
in making the green a quantity of bones and skulls were found in the
banked up side of the green closest to the shops.

In a match one day Kirkaldy's opponent was an eminent cleric who
was delighted to emerge from Hell bunker at the first attempt. His
pleasure was tempered when Kirkaldy remarked that he hoped he would
be as successful in after life. Kirkaldy died in 1934 and, as for his famous
predecessor, the draped silver clubs were carried at the funeral. At the
September meeting the following year Willie Auchterlonie, Open
Champion in 1893, was appointed professional to the Club.

In 1893, when he was 21, Auchterlonie won the Open championship
at Prestwick when Vardon and Taylor competed for the first time. His
victory, the most recent by a Scottish golfer domiciled in his own
country, was something of a surprise. Such was his tireless devotion to
club-making, in which he was apprenticed to the famous Forgan, that he
did not have as much time for practice as other leading players. Also his
experience was confined to the Old Course but a rare natural talent had
been developing since boyhood. Auchterlonie was powerful and the
'grasp of a vice' gave him an advantage with his long half-cleek approaches; he was a firm believer in the importance of the half and three-
quarter shot. The wet heavy conditions at Prestwick favoured his long,
carrying drive and, according to a contemporary account, he holed out
from six feet and under with machine-like regularity. He carried seven
clubs of his own making but used only five of them. Long afterwards
he was said to have referred to the modern game as a kind of ping-pong
played with an iron-monger's shop.

Auchterlonie impressed everyone at Prestwick, and throughout his
long life, by his composure under stress and by his reserved, modest
manner. He was a gentle person who was guided by stern, true prin-
ciples, taking everything, his dram and his tobacco, in moderation. In
many ways he was the antithesis of Kirkaldy. His reputation as a golfer
rested mainly on his Open victory but four years later his round of 71
became the record for the Old Course when playing with a gutty ball.
He must have been an uncommonly fine golfer and soon after his Open
victory he started his own business as a club-maker in St. Andrews
where his craft interested him more than playing. Auchterlonie re-

marked once that 'It's an awful empty life hitting golf balls every day; you are not giving much service.' This was his philosophy. Like others of his time he took great pride, not only in his skill, which had few peers, in fashioning beautiful clubs for individual players, but in serving the game and the Club.

In 1950, long after Auchterlonie had become a beloved figure at St. Andrews he, James Braid and J. H. Taylor were the first professional golfers to be made Honorary Members of the Royal and Ancient. The announcement at the September Meeting was warmly greeted by the Members who had subscribed to his portrait, painted by Macintosh Patrick, which hangs in the Clubhouse. Auchterlonie lived to see the Centenary Open in 1960 and died three years later in his 91st year.

Laurie Auchterlonie succeeded his father as Honorary Professional to the Club and inherited his skill as a clubmaker, his wisdom in the ways of the game and his sterling nature. As a young man he thought that he did not have the temperament to be a tournament golfer. Playing in the Amateur championship 'there were too many butterflies' before the matches and he decided that he must have a trade and so naturally he joined his father. This was before the age of steel shafts and mass production and he was blessed with a thorough foundation in the art of making clubs. So accomplished did he become that he made four sets for Bobby Jones as well as spare heads. In common with others of his generation he believed that with the coming of steel some of the skill went out of the game; the hickory shaft was a more sensitive instrument and needed greater control.

Like numerous young Scotsmen half a century ago, Auchterlonie was tempted to seek his fortune in the United States and he obtained a visa to go there, but he was an only son and his mother had died young. It was characteristic of the man that he did not leave his father. In time he became a leading authority on the history and making of early clubs and assembled a rare collection, including the work of great men like Philp and McEwan. In his later years he travelled frequently to the United States where his advice on many aspects of the game was sought and greatly respected.

Countless golfers make the pilgrimage to his shop around the corner from the Clubhouse. Apart from seeing his workshop and the beautiful examples of his craft they are rewarded by contact with a lively mind. His stimulating talk reveals a reverence for the past, the old players and the values they represented, but he is never lost in nostalgia. He regrets that he cannot recall the day when he was about four years old and Old

Tom Morris patted him on the head, but his father has assured him that this actually happened. The Royal and Ancient Club is fortunate that a man of Auchterlonie's charm and character is there as a cherished link with a distant age of golf.

CHAPTER ELEVEN

THE SECRETARY AND STAFF

The Second War marked the end of an era in the Club's history. In its first year the Captain, H. H. Sutherland, died and an interregnum of seven years was to follow. The Club also mourned the loss of Henry Gullen who had been Secretary for 28 years and a powerful influence in its affairs. He had travelled widely and was described as a great ambassador of golf. Among his possessions was a stand with seven Philp clubs which his widow presented to the Club.

The likelihood of war prompted Lord Wardington at a General Meeting in May 1939 to move that should it come an Emergency Committee be formed with powers to carry on the business of the Club. Members were drawn from those who were available from the General, House and Green Committees. Once the war had started Medal competitions, the Annual Dinner, and the Open and Amateur championships were cancelled.

A comparatively minor handicap endured by the golfers was that the manufacture of balls was forbidden, but the Club accumulated a 'Fund of Old Golf Balls' from which it made contributions to members of the Allied Forces. The Club was generous in its response to a letter from this writer in October 1943. A little golf course on sand had been fashioned in an Air Force prisoner-of-war camp at Sagan in eastern Germany but for some months the only available club was a hickory ladies' mashie. Fearing that it might break under the strain of hitting tens of thousands of shots the players sent appeals for clubs to neutral countries, and to the Royal and Ancient who sent clubs and balls through the Red Cross. It need hardly be said how greatly they were appreciated.

When at last the blackout could be removed from the Clubhouse windows and glass restored to the portraits, including those of the Prince of Wales, Earl Haig and Tom Morris, the Club resumed its peacetime ways. All the Medal competitions and the championships were held that summer.

Seemingly, professionals were regarded in that era with some sus-
picion. When there was a proposal to play a *Daily Mail* tournament
over the Old Course it was agreed that players might use the Clubhouse
but that they could only be served beer or mineral water. Whether this
was due to excessive caution or to shortage of supplies was not revealed
in the Minutes.

At about this time the Club declined an offer of a portrait of Morris
Cheape from Alexander Cheape of Strathtyrum, a house wherein hangs
the original of the famous picture, 'The Golfers'. The Cheape family
bought it in 1848 with the proviso that it was not to be sold unless the
proceeds were used for the provision of bread and water.

Among the numerous gifts received by the Club during this period
the most valuable was Golf Court, a building on the Scores, for use as a
Dormy House. It was given in memory of an R.A.F. officer killed in the
Battle of Britain, but a few years later the Club realised that it could
only be run at a loss. It was sold in 1952 for £10,000.

Meanwhile in 1946 J. A. Storer Carson had been chosen from some
150 candidates for the post of Secretary. When he resigned in 1952
Brigadier Eric Brickman was appointed in his stead. A man of quiet
charm and humour he gave fifteen years of devoted service to the Club
and won the affection and respect of everyone.

The organisation of the championships and the efficient working of
the Club in its many facets greatly depends on the permanent staff.
When Keith Mackenzie took over in 1967 it was clear that to a growing
extent the post needed a man of many parts and energies. Previously
Brickman and those before him had, with a minimum of staff, not only
guided the Club's internal affairs, but also, had organised the various
championships. That Brickman succeeded in doing so for several years
after the Open had begun to expand was a rare tribute to his endeavour.

The new Secretary needed the ability to organise and, particularly
where the Open was concerned, a knowledge of promotion, public
relations and business affairs. In this light he had to be accustomed to
command when necessary, and yet serve the Club in its ordinary ways.
As his duties would increasingly involve meeting people from every
walk of society and from many countries he would need to be sociable
and forthcoming. Mackenzie proved to be an admirable choice. Beneath
a genial manner there is a firm sense of purpose and a rare loyalty to the
stature of the Royal and Ancient. To golfers in the United States,
Australia, South Africa and many other countries Mackenzie must
appear to be a symbol of the Club. By no means the least of his services

has been to encourage overseas golfers to compete in the Open and to ensure that they are accommodated in Britain. In doing so he has been greatly responsible for the strength of the international entry which has no peer.

By 1979 the pressure upon the Club of daily administration, in addition to the effort needed to organise the championships, was such that the permanent Secretariat was revised and extended. Niel Loudon, the Deputy Secretary, became Secretary for External Affairs. This post continues to embrace his responsibility for matters relating to the Rules of Golf and the Rules of Amateur Status and, together with Keith Mackenzie, Loudon deals also with the numerous international and other governing bodies.

When the Championship Committee gathers in November one task is to choose the courses for the Open, and other events within its province, usually four years in advance. The long interval is necessary because throughout the seventies the production of the Open, and in a theatrical sense production it had almost become, was an increasingly complex and expensive undertaking.

Less than a generation ago providing facilities for the public hardly exercised the minds of the Committee at all. A few scattered 'comfort stations' were about the limit of their endeavours. As the Open expanded the siting of stands, seating eventually 17,000 people or more, score and progress boards, and a multitude of tents for a multitude of purposes; together with the provision of utilities, communication networks and so on involved much detailed planning. Apart from ensuring space, some 70 acres, for car parks (it was estimated that by 1978, when there were 9500 on the second day at St. Andrews, the number of visitors' cars had doubled from 13,000 overall in 1970) and various external activities, the first priority is the Open course and those used for qualifying rounds. Two years or more may be needed for the main course to be in the finest possible condition. To this end outside guidance is usually sought. Much of the credit for the revival of Turnberry from a poor state to admirable readiness for the 1977 Open was due to J. H. Arthur, an agronomist, whose advice on championship courses is sought by the Royal and Ancient.

Arrangements with local authorities, police, the numerous contractors involved, and the broadcasting companies are begun over a year in advance. Stand accommodation also is planned. Thenceforth the Championship Secretary, under the guidance of the Chairman and the Club Secretary, spends the greater part of his time on the Open. For many years he has been aided by the bustling, familiar figure of George Dunn, formerly of the Royal and New Zealand Navies. His tireless devotion in an abundance of tasks has become a byword. Whatever is needed 'Peg Leg', as he is affectionately called, usually finds or fixes it in his own individual way.

In the September prior to an Open the Championship Committee reviews the financial prospects and determines prize money and admission charges. The following April a local office is opened at the Open course, and some five weeks before it starts the Championship Secretary goes to live locally. George Wilson served in this capacity most capably until he was succeeded by David Hill towards the end of 1979. This was part of the extension to the Secretariat as a result of which George Wilson became Financial Secretary and Colin Scott assumed the new post of Members' Secretary.

The success of the Open depends in considerable measure on the co-operation and efficiency of the local Club's Championship Committee which is usually formed some two years beforehand. Among its tasks is the recruitment of staff and volunteers for numerous jobs such as car parks, scoreboard operation, litter removal and crowd control. In this last respect the Royal and Ancient were among the pioneers.

One of the first steps towards limiting spectators from following the golf on the fairways was taken by Norman Boase, Captain of the Club in 1935. He decreed that the first and last fairways at St. Andrews should be fenced and he was also responsible for the path through the whins from the 6th tee which became known as 'Boase Avenue'. After the Second War, M. E. Lindsay, a prominent figure in the Club's affairs, enlisted T. Rodger as Technical Officer for crowd control. For important events fencing and roping were increased, fairway crossings for spectators were made, and raised vantage points introduced. These were the fore-runners of stands. The primary purpose was to make watching more comfortable for spectators, and to reduce the problem of controlling large crowds on the Old Course narrowed by its double greens. Televising golf was years away and no-one realised how important it would then become to keep the fairways clear so that cameras could reveal the play to millions. As far back as 1954 G. W. Mackie had remarked on the possibility of stands but the Committee, fearing possible financial loss, had not agreed. In 1963 when, for the first time, a few stands were erected the cost of staging the Open, including prize money, was little more than £18,000. Ten years later this had multiplied almost twelve-fold and in 1978 the cost was well over £500,000.

CHAPTER TWELVE

THE MEMBERSHIP

Fifty years after the Society was formed Members were paying only five shillings annual subscription and half a guinea entrance fee, but in 1814 the subscription was raised to one guinea, and the proposer of a new Member had to pay the same amount. Some Members resigned in protest at a rule which if imposed nowadays would doubtless cause some proposers to think again.

The early Members were elected by ballot and two black balls were sufficient to bar them. The modern procedure is for a candidate to be proposed and seconded by Members. His name is then entered in the candidates book and circulated to all Members who may add their names in support or raise objections. If the candidate receives enough support to satisfy the Membership Committee his name goes on the waiting list. In extremely rare cases, such as that of President Ford, the Committee may accelerate membership. When a man becomes a Member and attends his first Annual Dinner after the Autumn Meeting he is expected to take part in an ancient ceremony which is still observed.

Writing of the Meeting in 1836 Thomas Frognall Dibdin describes how some eighty Members dined and how afterwards the Silver Club, 'which is used to propel the ball forward,' with the silver balls attached to it was placed before the Captain, Murray Belshes. The new Members then came forward in turn, raised the Club aloft and kissed one or more of the balls.

Then followed the Ball on the lower floor of the Town Hall where they had dined. Dibdin was impressed by the 'vigour and sprightliness throughout the whole' and the ladies reminded him of the days when there was pliancy in the limb, joy in the eye and delight in the dance.' Sadly, there have been no such occasions for admiration since the Ball was abandoned in 1937 but it may be revived. It had long been part of the Meeting; the Society held one in 1785 and a few years later there was a Fête Champêtre for the ladies.

One pleasant task of the General Committee is the power to invite people to become Honorary Members. Normally the distinction has fallen to Royalty, members of the Services and a few prominent citizens. Distinguished golfers were rarely included but in 1947, when the Walker Cup match was at St. Andrews, Francis Ouimet, captain of the American team, became the first eminent golfer from his country to be honoured. Nine years later the offer was made to Bobby Jones, already a Member, but while accepting he said that he wished to continue paying the annual subscription. Thus the most illustrious of all American amateurs were honoured, creating a further bond between the two countries.

In 1950 the Club wisely decided to recognise the contribution made over many years to the game in Britain and to the Open championship by professional golfers. James Braid, J. H. Taylor and Willie Auchterlonie accepted invitations, a proper tribute to men who by their character and skill had served the game nobly for a long time. Braid died soon afterwards and left one of his Open medals to the Club. When Taylor became 90 in 1961 Past Captains of the Club presented him with a salver bearing their signatures in honour of his birthday.

In time Walter Hagen, the first overseas professional to be invited, Arthur Havers, Bobby Locke, Gene Sarazen, Henry Cotton, Dai Rees, Roberto De Vicenzo and, most recently, Arnold Palmer became entitled to wear the tie. Their appreciation certainly matched that of Hagen who in 1968, the year before he died, wrote 'To say I was most pleased to receive your invitation to become an honorary member of the Royal and Ancient would be an understatement yet I simply cannot find the proper words to express my feelings for the Royal and Ancient who have so proudly carried their banner in the forefront of golf. At every opportunity I have urged our (U.S.) champions to play in Britain, telling them that they could never be complete champions until they have come face to face with the standards of golf set by great courses in Britain. Though I have not publicly been known for an excess of humility I can assure you that at this time it is with just such an emotion that I am pleased to accept your most gracious offer. Please extend my thanks to the chairman and members for their remembrance of me, Golfingly, Walter Hagen.'

At the Autumn Meeting in 1977 Henry Longhurst was made a Life Member. In accepting he said that he did not know whether to break into tears or buy drinks all round, but that on reflection he would do neither. Later in a letter he ended by saying 'I cannot believe that I shall ever make it to St. Andrews again but if that is so then this was certainly a wonderful leaving present.' He died the following summer having as a writer given more pleasure to more people than any Member since Bernard Darwin.

Honorary or Life Membership is not bestowed at random; neither is the Committee influenced by rank, social status or nationality. In 1951 a proposal to include two eminent persons from the Continent of Europe was rejected on the grounds that it might set an embarrassing precedent; so too was a suggestion that Foreign Ambassadors be honoured. In 1979 there were only nine Honorary Members of whom seven were professionals, thus reflecting the policy that service to golf was the principal qualification.

On one occasion the Club was caused some embarrassment over Honorary Membership. A letter, inspired by a malicious wit and purporting to be from an official of the Club, was sent to a famous person inviting him to become an Honorary Member. When he accepted the hoax came to light and considerable tact was required to withdraw the invitation but the explanation was accepted with good grace and the matter ended.

In 1974 the number of Members, apart from Honorary, was increased to 1800. Of the 750 overseas Members no more than 250 could be resident in the United States, and no more than 110 in any other country.

For the first time in its history the Club was faced in 1956 with the problem of a Member becoming a professional. For many years Frank Stranahan had been the most regular American competitor in British events; finishing second in the 1947 Open and winning the Amateur championship twice. When he turned professional it was suggested at the September Meeting that he should be asked to resign.

Apparently the subject was not raised again for some years. In the meantime Stranahan had won the Los Angeles Open as a professional. In 1959 the United States Golf Association were approached but as Stranahan was a Member of several of their affiliated clubs they were not prepared to take up the matter of his status with the Royal and Ancient. Eventually, three years later, Stranahan resigned and a rule was introduced to the effect that only an amateur golfer shall be eligible to become or remain a Member, unless Honorary.

The Royal and Ancient had no objection to professionals from other games being proposed for election. This came to light about the time that for cricketers the distinction between amateur and professional was abandoned.

CHAPTER THIRTEEN

THE CLUBHOUSE

The early golfers were not unaware of the social pleasures which could attend their game and probably regarded them as seriously as the golf itself. In May 1766 they bound themselves to meet once every fortnight and play a round of the links. This duty done they were further constrained to adjourn to Bailie Glass's House, an inn which probably became the Black Bull, and each pay one shilling for his dinner whether he was present or not. There is no evidence that Doctor Johnson took heed of golf during his visit to St. Andrews in 1773 but he and Boswell dined on haddock and mutton chops at Glass's.

No record exists of the talk which filled those evenings but the essence of it must have been similar to that which prompted James Balfour, a century later, to write that the humour of after-dinner conversations was 'positively sublime, you have heard squires at their wine after a good run, bless you they cannot hold a candle to golfers. How in the evening each dilates on his own wonderful strokes and the singular chances that befell him in the different parts of the green, all under the pleasurable delusion that every listener is as interested in his game as he is.'

Thus it has been and will ever remain so but the language of the 18th century was more graceful than it is now. One cannot imagine a golfer of those days coming in from his round and saying in the ghastly idiom of the modern tournament player 'I hit play-club real good out there, but three stabbed six times,' but they were probably human enough to blame their caddies for giving them the wrong lines.

Before 1835 the Club had no proper headquarters, holding its meetings at various taverns. Finally, the Cross Keys Inn, which still thrives, became the golfer's house but by then, largely through the influence of Sir Hugh Lyon Playfair, the Union Club was founded. It stood on land where, eventually, the Grand Hotel, now a University hostel, was built. The Union Club was started for the benefit of Members of the local Archers' Club and of the Golf Club, and in October 1853 it was decided that the Union Club and the Royal and Ancient should be united.

The necessity for a new Clubhouse had been foreseen in 1820 when the Town Council agreed that a piece of land be set aside should the Society wish to build. By 1853 the Union Club funds stood at over £800 and a Committee was formed to consider the project. An architect, Mr Rae, was appointed and plans approved by the Town Council. The estimated cost of the building, which occupied an area of 1567 square yards was less than £2000. John Whyte Melville was asked to lay the foundation stone but in the event Murray Belshes performed the task with full masonic honours. On Whit Sunday in 1854 the present Club-house was opened, almost exactly a century after the formation of what became the Royal and Ancient Club.

One provision of the design was that the walls of the large Hall, later known as the Big Room, were to be lined with wood to a height of six feet so that lockers could be arranged round the room. Also the great west window was to be lowered to within a foot of the floor. Eventually it was made into a bay window and these considerations doubtless were, and still are, blessed by generations of golfers as they look down the long sweep of the first and last holes to the woods and hills beyond.

It has on occasion been thought that, in common with other sporting bodies, the Club should administer its affairs from London but this has never been seriously considered. The fame of the Old Course and the atmosphere surrounding an ancient place, where so much of golfing history has been made, have attracted from all parts of the world, visitors who would not be drawn to an office in London with no golf course to hand. Thousands have been shown the Big Room and its portraits, and the museum with its miscellany of clubs, balls and trophies.

Some years ago the United States Golf Association retreated, thank-fully, from Manhattan to the peaceful countryside of New Jersey but it is not a Club whereas the Royal and Ancient is. Many of the Members are involved in administering the game, it is therefore fitting that the offices and permanent staff should be in the Clubhouse. Such were the increasing demands upon these resources, not only involving the interests of some 1800 Members from forty countries, but those of the Rules of Golf and the championships, that in 1979 considerable extensions to the Clubhouse were made. Happily these did not mar its outlines.

The beautiful handwriting in which many of the Club's early doings were recorded is an indication of the leisured pace of the times. Until late in the 19th century the Club's affairs were largely domestic; responsi-bility for the Rules of Golf and the championships was shared with others. The Management Committee, as it was then, the Secretary and Treasurer were able to look after the Members and the business of the Course.

These eminent figures were beset with such problems as the Members' dress. In 1820 it was decided that instead of their somewhat glamorous garb the uniform should be a plain blue coat with the Society's buttons. Hereabouts too there were recurring complaints that 'there is a considerable sum of entry money now in arrears of the Club,' a sentiment often echoed by club committees since.

In 1823 a Committee was appointed to superintend the Course. Four years later it had taken no action and was replaced by one of the local resident Members who appears to have been equally negligent, so the Club was forced to spend some money. In 1831 a Linkskeeper was employed at a salary of £5 which could be reduced if he proved inefficient. He survived until two members of the Herd family, both caddies, jointly took over with a raise of £1. Eventually Allan Robertson and Tom Morris were charged with keeping the green and the old haphazard methods, if indeed there were any, began to disappear.

Two of the most significant happenings in the 19th century coincided. The gutty ball appeared on the scene and the growth of the railway through Fife allowed golfers to reach St. Andrews by train. For the next hundred years and more they enjoyed the little journey from Leuchars, and a first sight of the links and the spires and dwellings of the old town. How eagerly they looked out at the golfers as the train scurried past the 15th and 16th fairways, how musical seemed the toot from the engine driver warning of arrival at St. Andrews, how sweet the knowledge that the Old Course would soon be their province.

When the railway was abandoned, supposedly in the cause of progress, and an unsightly hotel appeared in its stead the journey to St. Andrews, now an unmemorable drive, lost much of its appeal for those who remembered. Nonetheless the railway had helped to destroy the patrician and rather exclusive nature of golf, and to make it a game for all classes to play. St. Andrews, 'a retired place of learning and ecclesiastical leisure' had become more accessible, but the Club went its peaceful way relatively undisturbed.

The Committee made its decisions on many matters, as varied as imposing a fine of five shillings for bringing a dog into the Clubhouse and allowing Sir John Low the privilege granted to age of riding his cream coloured pony while playing the course. A century later the suggestion by an American Member that the rule regarding dogs should read 'no well-mannered dog shall be forbidden entrance to clubhouse' presumably did not find sufficient favour. The Committee decided that Members' old coats should be disposed of, the red ones to Tom Morris for cutting up into flags and the others to the inspector of the poor. The practice of Members putting their feet on tables was sternly discouraged. Count was taken of the complaint by sixteen Members who disliked the whisky provided by the Club, then twopence for a small glass, four-pence for a large one. If they preferred better quality they would have to pay $\frac{1}{2}$d and 1d more. At the same time iced water was to be available in the summer months, an enlightened move considering that there was no American influence.

Although the Club remained a resolutely masculine bastion its Members were still aware of their women folk. During the Meetings Members would take houses with their wives and families usually for three or four weeks but apart from the social round the women had much time on their hands while the men were playing and enjoying the Club. The women reacted in the most appropriate fashion in 1867 by forming the St. Andrews Ladies Club and such was the enthusiasm that within twenty years they had 500 members. The putting green north-east of the Swilcan Burn and the 2nd tee on the Old became their particular battleground and remains so. Regular meetings are held and their many handsome prizes include a Gold Medal and a Silver Cross.

This activity by the distaff side did not involve any closer union with the Club. After a lapse of almost twenty years attempts were made in the fifties to revive the Annual Ball and finally in 1959 it seemed that all was set fair for it to be held during the September Meeting. The Younger Hall of the University was booked and a band engaged. 250 tickets at three guineas each would have to be sold to cover costs but three days before the event only 141 had gone so the Ball was cancelled.

When the British Ladies Championship was played on the Old Course in 1975, and competitors and officials were given the courtesy of the Clubhouse, two Members resigned in protest, but more liberal attitudes were prevailing. In January 1976 a mixed buffet evening was held in the Clubhouse and this proved so popular that it became neces-sary to hold two astride the turn of each year.

CHAPTER FOURTEEN

THE MUSEUM

The Museum in the South Room of the Clubhouse owed its origin to an Admiral Bethune who in 1864 suggested that the Committee should form a collection of such articles as would preserve a record of remarkable matches and incidents. The outcome is a selection of clubs and balls covering two centuries of the game's growth, from a play-club, probably the oldest of its kind, made by Samuel Cosser in 1760, to those of the present age.

Notable among the wooden clubs which preceded the use of irons are those made by several generations of the McEwan family. The firm, started by James late in the 18th century, continued making clubs for over a century and the Royal and Ancient has examples of every period. The McEwans began business in Edinburgh but as golf moved down the coast they opened their main branch in Musselburgh. In their survey of 'Golf in the Making' Ian Henderson and David Stirk tell how, early in the 19th century, the McEwans were paid an annual fee of two guineas for David Robertson, their agent in St. Andrews and the father of the famous Allan, to attend the Spring and Autumn Meetings.

This enterprising practice ceased in 1827 because in 1819 the Society, not then the Royal and Ancient, had appointed Hugh Philp as its official clubmaker in succession to a certain Fraser. The Club now has probably the finest collection in the world of his work. Philp was a quiet man, simple and natural in manner with a 'fine eye for a club and exquisite tastes'. He soon gained a great reputation for his clubs and it was said that they were to a golfer what a Toledo blade was to a swordsman.

His putters were famous and in later years commanded high prices. In his history Hugo Everard, writing in 1906, recalled being offered £5 for one, a sum comparable with those which can snare modern golfers into the delusion that money can buy a true putting stroke. When Philp died in 1856 his nephew, Robert Forgan, who had previously been taken into the business, succeeded him and his firm became equally famous. Many clubmakers, notably Willie Auchterlonie, learned their skills from him and for over a century the Forgan shop overlooked the 18th on the Old Course.

In many ways golf was a more adventurous pastime in the old days. For instance players would try their hand at making clubs and balls. The latter were relatively expensive to buy and Thomas Peter wrote that 'For long I made my own balls at small cost. My brother and I succeeded in inserting lead in the centre of the ball so that it putted accurately'. This might have been so but it was done at some cost to the clubs. They were often damaged to the vexation of Philp who, on seeing his beautiful handiwork ruined, remarked 'How the devil can a man make a club to stand against lead?'

The various niblicks in the Museum reveal the inventiveness of the clubmaker before rules restrained imagination. Willie Auchterlonie had great faith in his wooden niblick, somewhat like a spoon in loft, and doubtless many tried to escape from the Swilcan or similar affliction by using a niblick with a hole in the face to ease its passage through water. Those who marvelled at Walter Hagen's dexterity in playing from sand might be less impressed if they saw the weapon he used. Its face is almost as concave as that of a huge soup spoon. Ingenuity in the fashioning of putters is far from recent. One in the Museum is shaped like a stamping iron, another, probably the only one in existence, is of brass with a peculiar lip on the sole. On the other hand a Dutch putter made in 1800, with a simple blade head, would suffice now except for the thickness of the grip, a common feature of the old clubs.

Famous clubs of famous men also stir memories. The driver used by Allan Robertson when he became the first man to break 80 on the Old Course is here; so also is a hickory shafted set which helped Bobby Jones win some of his championships. The driver with which Francis Ouimet drove himself in as Captain is displayed, together with the five iron which despatched Gene Sarazen's tee shot into the 8th hole at Troon in the first round of the 1973 Open.

Apart from the implements in the Museum there is evidence elsewhere in the Club of the generosity of Members, other individuals and of governing bodies. Among these are a Persian carpet from The Abadan Golf Club and a cloisonne vase from the Economic Mission of the Japanese Embassy which was given in 1937, long before golf became a passion in Japan. The reasoning that governs the acceptance of gifts is not always clear. In 1892 the Club accepted with thanks from K. L. Keyser a ball said to have been chewed, swallowed and evacuated by a cow. Many years later the offer of a Louis XIV clock 'would be considered after being examined by the Committee'. It appears that either the clock did not pass their scrutiny or that the donor withdrew his offer.

CHAPTER FIFTEEN

HOMAGE TO A PEERLESS GOLFER

During the Spring Meeting in 1972 a long romance between a golfer and a golfing place drew to a close with a memorial service to Robert Tyre Jones in the Holy Trinity Church of St. Andrews. After years of suffering from a grievous affliction Jones had died the previous December. The Service was arranged as a final tribute from St. Andrews and the Royal and Ancient to the supreme golfer of his time, a person of rare gifts and an Honorary Member of the Club.

There had never been an affinity between a great golfer from overseas and a British links comparable to that of Jones and St. Andrews, although long years later the same probably was true of Jack Nicklaus. In 1927 Jones won the second of his three Open championships in Britain with what was then a record score; three years later he was Amateur champion and had passed the first stage of his journey on the way to the ultimate peak of achievement for an amateur golfer.

Several times during that championship in 1930 the destiny of the 'Grand Slam' hung on a thread. Mention of the famous match with Cyril Tolley has been made elsewhere in this narrative and there were other occasions when Jones was sorely pressed. In the semi-final he was two down after thirteen holes and fortunate that George Voigt drove out of bounds at the 14th, and into the Principal's Nose at the 16th. Over 36 holes Jones was wellnigh invincible. His morning round in the final, during which he had only one five, gave him unshakeable command over Wethered. On his return home Jones received a miniature of the Trophy bearing the inscription, 'To Robert Tyre Jones Jr., a golfer matchless in skill and chivalrous in spirit, from some fellow members of the Royal and Ancient Club.'

Jones was the only man who had won both championships at St. Andrews, a distinction he is likely to hold for evermore. His respect and affection for the Old Course and the Club became famous throughout the golfing world. Aside from his pleasure in the victories Jones had come to love the ancient subtleties of the links which had frustrated him on his first visit in 1921.

Six years after his retirement from championship golf Jones returned to St. Andrews expecting to play a quiet friendly game. Although it had been arranged at short notice word had spread like fire through the town and, to his astonishment, some two thousand people had gathered before he started, a remarkable tribute. His form had not been too good previously but the atmosphere inspired him. He played with Willie Auchterlonie, the Club's professional, and as the crowds grew he reached the turn in 32. Unfortunately he overhit the 11th green and took five, and a little of the magic left him but he finished with a three and was round in 72. This was his last golf on the Old Course, but not his last memorable experience at St. Andrews.

When Jones came for the first World Amateur Team Championship he could only walk a little with the aid of sticks and he followed the golf in an electric cart. During the practice he moved about the course, reminiscently as might a man returning after many years to an old and beloved garden, doubtless he was recalling shots he had played and the moments of triumph and anxiety. He noticed any slight changes to the holes, including the little bunker that had trapped him behind the 11th green. Even the head greenkeeper was not aware that it had once been there. Throughout those days people would approach to pay their homage, the old ones who remembered and the young who wished they had known the beauty of his golf.

The championship was agonisingly close and one memory of the climax will never perish. William Hyndman was playing last for the United States, and as he stood on the 17th fairway in the fourth round it seemed certain that he had to finish with two fours, or even better, if his side were to survive. Jones had told his men that they must never play for the top level of the green, wise counsel in a team medal event, but the situation then was desperate. Hyndman looked across at Jones, sitting in his cart nearby, and indicated that he wanted to attempt the shot. Jones nodded agreement and Hyndman responded with as fine a stroke under severe pressure as St. Andrews had seen in many a year. His four iron shot bored through the deepening twilight to within five feet of the hole and his courage was rewarded when the putt fell for a three.

In September that year the Town Clerk of St. Andrews had cabled Jones asking him to accept the Freedom of the City. The Ceremony in the Younger Graduation Hall of the University, was held on the second evening of the championship. It was the most emotional occasion that this writer has known in golf, as it probably was for the 1700 who filled the Hall. Had the building been larger two or three times as many people would have been there. The Provost of St. Andrews Robert Leonard welcomed Jones not only as a distinguished golfer but as a man of outstanding character, courage and accomplishment well worthy to adorn the Roll of Honorary Burgesses. The last American thus honoured had been Doctor Benjamin Franklin almost two centuries earlier.

In making his reply Jones, who spoke as he wrote with an ease and grace given to precious few players of games, had no need of the notes he had prepared. He likened the Old Course to a 'wise old lady, whimsically tolerant of my impatience, but ready to reveal the secrets of her complex being, if I would only take the trouble to study and learn'.

How many golfers in their struggles to master the course must have realised the truth of this. Whether they could act upon it was another matter. Jones said that the more he studied the course the more he loved it, and that he came to appreciate that it was for him the most favourable meeting ground for an important contest. 'I felt that my knowledge of the course enabled me to play it with patience and restraint until she might exact her inevitable toll from my adversary, who might treat her with less respect and understanding.' Nicklaus might well echo these words.

Jones went on to speak of friendship. 'When I say, with due regard for the meaning of the word, that I am your friend, I have pledged to you the ultimate in loyalty and devotion. In some respects friendship may even transcend love, for in true friendship there is no place for jealousy. When, without more, I say that you are my friends, it is possible that I may be imposing upon you a greater burden than you are willing to assume. But when you have made me aware on many occasions that you have a kindly feeling toward me, and when you have honoured me by every means at your command, then when I call you my friend, I am at once affirming my high regard and affection for you and declaring my complete faith in you and trust in the sincerity of your expressions. And so, my fellow citizens of St. Andrews, it is with this appreciation of the full sense of the word that I salute you as my friends.'

Towards the end of his speech Jones said 'I could take out of my life everything except my experiences at St. Andrews and I would still have a rich full life'. It was small wonder that the people worshipped him. A few moments later his son helped him into his cart and as he and the Provost rode down the Hall together the people began to sing, 'Will Ye No Come Back Again'. It was a deeply moving moment with a deadly finality to it. Everyone knew that St. Andrews would never see him, or anyone like him, again. Herbert Warren Wind and I left the Hall together and some minutes passed before either of us could trust his voice.

It was hard to believe then that Jones would live for another thirteen years. The cruel disease of the spine took terrible toll of his body that became ever more harrowing to see, but an unquenchable spirit, a splendid, cultured mind and sense of humour enabled him to survive. He inspired the admiration and affection of golfers everywhere but he was in the words of Al Laney, one of America's most perceptive observers of the game, 'an ancient game's greatest champion, an extraordinary human being of exceeding talents reaching far beyond his incomparable sporting feats'.

Twelve Captains of the Royal and Ancient attended the Memorial Service at St. Andrews and Roger Wethered, the senior among them, who had played so often with Jones, gave the address. It was a peaceful, gentle time as befitted an uncommonly gentle man.

BIBLIOGRAPHY

A History of the Royal and Ancient Golf Club, H. S. C. Everard (Blackwood, 1907).

The Story of the Royal and Ancient, J. B. Salmond (Macmillan, 1956).

The Badminton Library (Longmans Green, 1890).

A History of Golf in Britain (Cassell, 1952).

A History of Golf, Robert Browning (Dent, 1955).

Golf is my Game, Robert T. Jones (Doubleday, 1960).

Muirfield and the Honourable Company, George Pottinger (Scottish Academic Press, 1972).

St. Andrews, Douglas Young (Cassell, 1969).

Reminiscences of Golf on St. Andrews Links, James Balfour (1870?).

The Life of Tom Morris, W. W. Tulloch (T. Werner Laurie, 1908).

Fifty Years of Golf, Horace Hutchinson (Country Life, 1919).

The Story of American Golf, Herbert Warren Wind (Knopf, 1975).

Thirty Years of Championship Golf, Gene Sarazen (Prentice Hall, 1950).

Golf Courses of the British Isles, Bernard Darwin (Duckworth, 1910).

USGA Record Book (Published by USGA).

Golfers Gallery, Frank Moran (Oliver and Boyd, 1946).

Fifty Years of Golf, My Memories, Andrew Kirkaldy (Unwin, 1921).

Scotland's Gift: Golf; Reminiscences, Charles Blair Macdonald (Scribners, 1928).

The author is grateful to J. Stewart Lawson, Captain of the Club, W. M. Miller, R. Macleod and G. H. Micklem who read the manuscript; W. N. B. Loudon for his guidance regarding the Rules of Golf; K. R. T. Mackenzie and his staff for their help, and the Editors of *Country Life* and *The Guardian* for reference to their journals.